All About
HOUSEPLANTS

Created and designed by the editorial staff of ORTHO Books

Project Editor Barbara J. Ferguson ∾ *Writer* Susan M. Lammers

Designer James Stockton ∾ *Major Photographers* Fred Lyon, Michael McKinley

Ortho Books

Publisher
Robert L. Iacopi

Editorial Director
Min S. Yee

Managing Editors
Anne Coolman
Michael D. Smith
Sally W. Smith

Production Manager
Ernie S. Tasaki

Editors
Jim Beley
Susan Lammers
Deni Stein

Design Coordinator
Darcie S. Furlan

System Managers
Christopher Banks
Mark Zielinski

Photographic Director
Alan Copeland

Photographers
Laurie A. Black
Richard A. Christman

Production Editors
Linda Bouchard
Alice Mace
Kate O'Keeffe

Asst. System Manager
William F. Yusavage

Chief Copy Editor
Rebecca Pepper

Photo Editors
Anne Dickson-Pederson
Pam Peirce

National Sales Manager
Garry P. Wellman

Sales Associate
Susan B. Boyle

Operations Director
William T. Pletcher

Operations Assistant
Gail L. Davis

Administrative Assistant
Georgiann Wright

Address all inquiries to
Ortho Books
Chevron Chemical Company
Consumer Products Division
575 Market Street
San Francisco, CA 94105

Chevron Chemical Company
575 Market Street, San Francisco, CA 94105

Color Separations
Color Tech Corp.
Redwood City, California

Illustrator
Kirk Caldwell

Location researcher
Diane Saeks

Manuscript consultants
Dr. Charles C. Powell
Columbus, Ohio

Dr. Kenneth Horst
Ithaca, New York

Manuscript/Gardening Editor
Frank Shipe

Photographers
(Names of photographers in
alphabetical order are followed by
page numbers on which their work
appears. R = right, C = center, L =
left, T = top, and B = bottom.)

M. Baker: 19L, 19R

John Blaustein: 37

Clyde Childress: 52

Josephine Coatsworth: 55

Michael Lamotte: Title page, back
cover

Michael Landis: 36, 49B

Fred Lyon: Front cover, 4, 6, 8, 22, 24,
25, 26, 27, 28, 29, 30T, 30B, 31T, 31B,
32T, 32L, 33T, 33B, 34, 43, 46, 54

Michael McKinley: 7T, 7B, 20C, 21C,
53R, 53L, and the entire "Gallery of
Houseplants" except for 62R, 62B,
64B

James McNair: 39L

Picnic Productions: 11L

Dr. Robert Raabe, University of
California, Berkeley, CA: 64B

Anita Sabarese: 62B, 62R

Typography
Vera Allen Composition
Castro Valley, California

Special Thanks
We are especially grateful to the
following persons and companies for
allowing us to photograph their
homes, their offices, and their
houseplants.

Bill and Barbara Belloli
San Francisco, CA

Conservatory of Flowers
Golden Gate Park, San Francisco, CA

East Bay Nursery
Berkeley, CA

Esprit de Corp
San Francisco, CA

Fern Hollow
Oakland, CA

Scott Lamb
San Francisco, CA

Rod McClellan Co. (Acres of Orchids)
South San Francisco, CA

Sloat Garden Center
Mill Valley, CA

Robert Steffi
San Francisco, CA

Jim Stockton
San Francisco, CA

Michael Tedrick/Thomas Bennett
Interior Design, San Francisco, CA

The Greenhouse on Union Street
San Francisco, CA

Tommy's Plants
San Francisco, CA

Front cover: Every plant in this
display can be found in the "Gallery
of Houseplants", the final chapter of
the book.

Back cover: *Davallia mariesii*,
squirrel's foot fern or ball fern.

Title page: Author Susan Lammers
pots up colorful spring-blooming
primroses.

All About
HOUSEPLANTS

BRINGING NATURE INDOORS

The intrigue and appeal of growing plants indoors ❧ Why certain plants become houseplants ❧ A modern approach to an age-old hobby

As highways, highrises, shopping centers, and all of the other concrete and steel creations of civilization spread into the countryside—supplanting meadows, woods, farms, and gardens—people have found a renewed awareness of the need to be in close contact with nature and have acted upon it.

The most obvious sign of this has been the extraordinary surge in the practice of bringing nature indoors. In the last decade alone, millions of people in this country have taken up growing houseplants.

Undoubtedly the sense of security and tranquility commonly felt and enjoyed by so many when surrounded by plants comes from being so dependent on them for survival. Almost every aspect of our daily lives involves plants: They supply the oxygen we breathe, the clothes we wear, the food we eat, the materials we use to shelter ourselves, even the paper upon which this book is printed. Bringing plants indoors allows us to nurture and maintain a close relationship with a primary source of life.

It's a small wonder we cherish houseplants so much in our indoor environment. Nothing adds warmth and visual excitement to a decor quite as well as vigorous plants. Their tranquility and graceful beauty help make a house or apart-

Kalanchoe blossfeldiana, known as flaming Katy, welcomes you indoors with its scarlet flowers. This hardy succulent thrives in bright light.

ment into a home. From the smallest child to the oldest adult, everyone enjoys watching plants grow and blossoms unfold. While their beauty and vitality delight everyone, for the person who tends them indoor gardening provides immense gratification and pleasure.

People have been cultivating plants indoors for thousands of years. Long ago, the Egyptians, Assyrians, Babylonians, Chinese, Greeks, Romans, Incas, Aztecs, and countless other civilizations put plants in containers and brought them onto terraces and into their homes. By the early 18th century more than 5,000 species of tropical and semitropical plants were in cultivation indoors all over the world. During the 19th century, improvements in plant transportation methods made even more species widely available, especially to the Victorian English, who were enthralled with growing plants everywhere—in greenhouses and conservatories, parlors, bedchambers, sunrooms, and libraries.

People still are enthralled with displaying plants indoors, but no longer do we find many homes decorated in the ostentatious, formal manner so popular with the Victorians. The plants we grow are much more numerous and diverse and include countless hybrids different from those they grew. The ways we display them reflect our simpler modern tastes and the need to blend our houseplants with contemporary interior designs. Today,

we see kitchen windows brimming with potted begonias, or living rooms graced by ficus trees. Hanging baskets of grape ivy, philodendrons, and Boston ferns decorate many windows. And in interior spaces where sunlight never reaches, fluorescent and directed incandescent lights provide life-giving rays for plants.

WHAT IS A HOUSEPLANT?

Houseplants differ from outdoor plants only in terms of their location. They were not originally developed to grow indoors; rather, many were derived from ancestors native to the shade of tropical forests. In this habitat temperature changes are seasonal, heavy rainfall and high humidity are normal, and the ground is rich in nutrients from decayed leaves shed by the thick vegetation. Houseplants are wild plants that have been domesticated.

The plants selected as houseplants share one feature in common—adaptability. They can endure the filtered light and moderate fluctuations in temperature and humidity that occur in our homes. Yet in some ways they continue to behave as if they were growing in an outdoor environment.

One indication that houseplants retain their innate characteristics becomes most apparent during autumn and winter, when many plants enter a period of dormancy or rest. Despite their placement indoors, many plants will lose some leaves. And no matter how humid

it is or how often you water a cactus, it will always hoard food as if it were in the desert. Old habits may recede in new environments, but they must be taken into account.

Some plants are naturally short-lived, dying with the onset of fall or winter. Regardless of whether environmental conditions reflect the change in seasons, the genetic structure of the plant simply dictates a short life span. The sensitive plant is a good example.

Hundreds of thousands of plant species thrive all over the earth. Those cultivated as houseplants are the most beautiful of the most tolerant; they can adjust to a human environment. Plants do, however,

have certain needs that we don't have; and learning, understanding, and satisfying these needs is the challenge of indoor gardening.

In the past, many books written about houseplants have relied on old-fashioned methods and traditional indoor gardening techniques. But much has changed since the Victorian Age, when houseplants first became widely popular, and life continues to change at an ever-increasing pace. Today we know more about plant cultivation. New techniques are available that enable us to grow more plants indoors and keep them healthier without taking too much time out of our own busy schedules.

The purpose of this book is to give you an understanding of plants and up-to-date information on selecting them and caring for them in the contemporary home environment. In "Houseplant Basics," starting on page 9, you'll see exactly how plants grow and how light, temperature, and humidity affect them—everything you need to know in order to understand the care requirements of your indoor plants. If you've ever been puzzled by problem areas in your decor or wondered where to put plants to the best effect, "Creating the Indoor Landscape," starting on page 23, will tell you how to design with houseplants. This section covers everything from basic concepts to special situations, and includes many photographic examples.

"Day-to-Day Care," page 35, will give you the details of care and special tips to keep your plants in the peak of health. You'll also learn how to grow plants under artificial light.

"Propagation," page 47, will show you how to increase your houseplant collection easily and inexpensively. In no time you'll be trading cuttings and exchanging information with others who share your enthusiasm for indoor gardening.

The major portion of this book, "The Gallery of Houseplants," starting on page 55, is an invaluable guide for beginners and experienced indoor gardeners alike. It lists over 100 of the most popular houseplants best suited to growing in our homes. You'll find hard facts on culture, complete descriptions, and photographs that will help you select and grow the best plants for your needs.

Reading this book will never replace the pleasure of growing an indoor garden, but it serves as a source of ideas and practical information to help you on your way to growing beautiful plants.

Opposite: A mature Ficus benjamina 'Exotica' graced by blooming cape primroses and a bird's nest fern provides a striking focal point in this room. Above: Place your African violets near a mirror to double the amount of color and increase the light. Below: The delicate Chinese primrose blooms in winter.

HOUSEPLANT BASICS

Understanding plant growth ❧ Leaf, root, stem, and flower functions ❧
Selecting houseplants ❧ Planting your own hanging baskets and terrariums

To the beginning indoor gardener, and even those with some experience, caring for houseplants can be a mysterious and even slightly disconcerting project. For many of us, the following is all too familiar:

One day you go out to shop for groceries and the next thing you know you're in the checkout line buying a beautiful houseplant you just couldn't pass up. Welcoming your new friend into your home, you water it, set it on a sunny window sill, talk to it, and then wait anxiously for it to grow and possibly blossom. Somehow, instead of bringing the lush growth you expect, all your tender loving care works awry: the leaves droop, the color fades, and any buds it has begin to drop. This dismal turn sends you into a mild panic—you pour on more water and fertilizer and cart the plant around the house trying new locations.

Your plant may recover, but chances are that this random treatment, however well-intentioned, will not be exactly what it needs and will prove unsuccessful—and most unrewarding for you.

Just what are the best ways to keep a plant alive and healthy? Exactly what should you do for the houseplants in your home, and why? Watering, fertilizing, grooming, propagating, and seasonal care—often bewildering when first considered—are easy to carry out properly once you know exactly

Repotting encourages vigorous growth.

how they affect plants. For this, all you need is an understanding of the basic processes of plant growth and survival.

PHOTOSYNTHESIS: STORING ENERGY

The fertilizers you buy to make your plants grow well are often called "plant food," but in fact they're not really food because they don't produce energy. However, fertilizers do contain substances plants need to carry out life processes, and in this respect they're supplements, just as vitamins are supplements to our nutrition.

Like all living beings, the food that plants actually use as a source of energy is *sugar*, but unlike other living organisms, plants themselves manufacture their own sugar through the marvelous process of *photosynthesis.*

In photosynthesis, light, chlorophyll, energy, carbon dioxide, and water act together within the plant to produce the sugar and release oxygen. Plants harness the sun's energy to stimulate this process and it will take place only when they are in the presence of light. What happens, very simply, is this:

Plant leaves draw in carbon dioxide from the atmosphere and roots absorb water from the soil. The chlorophyll in the leaves and other green tissues absorbs the light energy and uses it to split the water into hydrogen and oxygen. The hydrogen and carbon dioxide immediately combine into sugar and the

oxygen is given off into the surrounding atmosphere.

It's worth noting that the oxygen this process frees into the air makes up all of the oxygen we breathe. And the role of photosynthesis becomes even grander when you consider that it not only provides us oxygen, but by converting sunlight into chemical energy, it produces the energy that sustains all plant and animal life on earth.

For photosynthesis to occur, a plant's leaves, stems, and roots must be healthy and interacting properly in a favorable environment, meaning one with adequate light, temperature, and humidity. It's especially important to note that because this process is a plant's only source of food and fertilizers are just supplements, no amount of fertilizer or number of applications can ever make up for any improper environment or care that would slow down or stop it. Maximum plant health and growth require maximum rates of photosynthesis.

Plant care becomes much simpler when you realize that it is largely a matter of providing the elements that allow photosynthesis to take place. If you do this, your plants will thrive; if you don't, you are bound to watch your plants decline.

The role of photosynthesis, then, is to make food for the plant. When it produces more food than the plant can use immediately, the excess is stored for later use. How the plant uses food brings us to another major process.

RESPIRATION: SUPPLYING ENERGY

Respiration is the process in which the sugar made in photosynthesis is combined with oxygen and, in a sense, "burned" to release energy and heat. This reaction also produces carbon dioxide and water, which the plant then gives off into the air. The plant uses the energy respiration releases to maintain its life and produce new cells for growth.

In many ways respiration is the reverse of photosynthesis. In photosynthesis, plants absorb carbon dioxide and water, make food, and give off oxygen; in respiration, plants absorb oxygen, break down food, and give off carbon dioxide and water. Photosynthesis stores energy; respiration frees it. Photosynthesis takes place only in light; respiration is active both day and night because plants need a steady supply of energy. A plant therefore does its growing both day and night, whereas it is manufacturing food only during the day.

Because respiration cannot occur without food, it follows that the same factors that encourage photosynthesis encourage respiration.

TRANSPIRATION

The heat produced in respiration can build up within a plant when coupled with warm temperatures. On a sunny day the temperature inside a leaf can be as much as 10°F higher than that of the surrounding air. Yet, like animals, plants must maintain a healthy heat and moisture balance to live and function efficiently. They do this through the process of *transpiration*.

Transpiration cools by evaporation. Similar to the release of sweat from your body, water vapor exits the plant from leaf pores (called *stomata*) when they open to absorb the gases necessary in photosynthesis and respiration. If you have ever been in a forest on a hot summer day, the coolness you feel there is not only because of the shade, but also because water is being transpired by the multitudes of leaves

that are all around you.

The rate of transpiration depends on the surrounding air's temperature and humidity. The higher the temperature and the lower the humidity, the faster plants transpire, and the more water they give off. If they transpire more water than they can absorb through the roots, they will wilt.

Transpiration plays another crucial role in plant life. As the plant releases water vapor from the leaves, more water is drawn up to replace it. This produces the vital flow of water and nutrients absorbed by the roots throughout the plant.

Indoors, plants are often subject to variable light conditions and to high temperatures and very low humidity. In containers they have access to a limited supply of water. All of these factors affect photosynthesis, respiration, and transpiration. The importance of controlling them in order to achieve sustained health and maximum growth cannot be stressed enough.

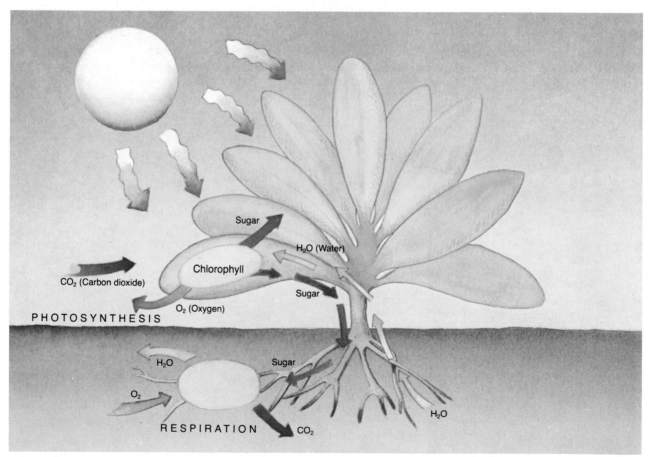

Sugars produced in photosynthesis move to the various parts of the plants where they are needed. There they are converted into energy for growth through the process of respiration.

THE PARTS OF THE PLANT

There are four major parts of a plant: roots, stems, leaves, and flowers. All are crucial to plant life and are worth special attention.

The Roots

The roots serve two important functions:They anchor the plant and absorb the water and mineral elements that nourish it. Most of this absorption occurs through root tips and the tiny root hairs found on young roots. These root hairs develop in minute spaces among soil particles, where oxygen, minerals, and water are held.

Unlike the older, tougher roots, new roots and root hairs are extremely delicate and easily injured. Transplanting often destroys most of them and even though the major root system may remain intact, this causes the top of the plant to wilt. In proper conditions, however, new root hairs will grow within a few days to replace those destroyed.

Roots absorb only as much water as the plant needs. Too much water will displace oxygen from the soil, suffocating the roots. Far too many houseplants die from well-intentioned overwatering, especially when pots lack adequate drainage. (At this point you may be wondering how a houseplant cutting can root directly in water, a commonplace way of starting new plants. The answer is that the cutting develops specialized roots capable of deriving oxygen from water. Not all plants develop these roots, however, and those that do often have difficulty when transplanted because they must then expend energy to form new roots adapted to the soil.)

Roots also serve to store food and send water and nutrients to the stem to start their distribution to other parts of the plant.

The Stem

The stem transports the water and minerals to the leaves, buds, and flowers, and also distributes the food produced in photosynthesis. In addition it physically supports the plant and serves to store food when unsuitable growing conditions prevail and through the dormant period until time to initiate growth in the spring.

Most houseplants, including many that climb or trail, have herbaceous, or nonwoody, stems.

The Leaf

The leaf is responsible for manufacturing the plant's food through photosynthesis. The large surface area and thinness of the leaf suit this purpose very well, allowing for the maximum absorption of light.

On the underside of the leaf are thousands of stomata that expand or contract in response to environmental and physiological conditions. The large surface area of the leaf and the action of the stomata make possible the most efficient absorption and diffusion of gases and water vapor.

Leaves also can absorb minerals and other nutrients directly from the air or from direct applications of certain fertilizers; and they are crucial in the process of transpiration described earlier.

The Flower

The flower contains the plant's reproductive apparatus. The colors, shapes, and scents of flowers serve to attract butterflies, bees, hummingbirds, and other pollinating creatures. Although all plants can flower in a natural environment, only some do indoors, where the environment is not always conducive to flower production.

Roots—an underground growth network.

Fuchsia leaves manufacture sugars, the food plants use to produce flowers.

LIGHT

Light is a critical factor in growing plants indoors. Without adequate light plants cannot photosynthesize enough food for growth to occur. As an indoor gardener you should consider both the amount of light available and the length of time it is present in your home.

The *intensity* and the *duration* of light both vary considerably within a home, not only from room to room but also within one room. For example, light is less intense at a window with shades or curtains than at an unobstructed window. In the same room another window may permit more intense light to enter, but for a shorter time. Light at a single window will vary in intensity and duration if trees or other obstructions outside block the sun's rays at certain times of day. Furniture and reflective surfaces within a room can alter light as well. All of the conditions in your home that affect light should be taken into consideration when you set out to raise houseplants.

Most houseplants benefit from receiving as much indirect light as possible, rather than direct sun. Only a few benefit from more than 1 to 2 hours of direct sun in the summer. This direct sunlight and the intense heat that often accompanies it can be extremely harmful to your plants.

Seasonal Light

With different seasons the angle of the sun changes, so intensity varies. Summer sun shines almost perpendicular to the earth, striking it with maximum intensity. In contrast, our winter sun hovers low in the sky, even at noon. Its rays travel on a slanted path and consequently pass through more dust and moisture in the air, which scatters or diffuses the light, reducing its intensity. At noon on a clear day in midsummer, when the sun shines directly overhead, the level of illumination is much higher than it is in December. On a rainy day in winter it may be only one twentieth the light intensity of summer. Given this reduced intensity, it's easy to understand why so many plants grow very slowly during the colder months of the year.

Even the most tender African violet or begonia will welcome full winter sun. However, in the warmer seasons the situation changes and you should be cautious about the amount of light that reaches your plants.

All of the care you give your plants must coincide with the seasonal increases and decreases in light intensity. During summer when light is brightest and heat is highest, all plant life processes speed up and plants absorb more water, more minerals, and more carbon dioxide. Therefore, you must provide them with more moisture and fertilizer. During winter, when light is less intense and photosynthesis slows, a cutback in moisture and fertilizer is in order.

Where you live also affects how much light you receive. For example, sunlight in the Rockies during winter is much more intense than in New England because the higher elevation means thinner air and less light diffusion through the atmosphere. In winter, the sun rises and sets farther to the south of the United States. Consequently Florida and other southern states receive more bright light than northern states such as Montana.

Even within your local area light intensity will vary, and not just because of the seasons. Smoke from local industry may make sunny days hazy. Clouds or fog will cut down light. Trees and shrubs that shade your home reduce the amount of light that passes through your windows. Screened windows, doors, or porches reduce light by as much as 30 percent. A white house next door or a light-color cement driveway will reflect sunlight, increasing the intensity of light your rooms receive. Snow will reflect a great deal of light, especially on a sunny day.

Too little light causes a plant to elongate and lose leaves that it can no longer support due to diminished photosynthesis. As the plant attempts to gather more light, the spaces on the stems between the leaves (called *internodes*) lengthen and the leaves grow broad and thin. You can correct a low light situation in several ways. Increasing the duration of light helps compen-

Rotate plants that lean toward light.

sate for low intensity, so simply move the plant to a window that admits light for a longer time. Or you can supplement daylight with artificial light (see page 38). However, these changes will help only if the added light is intense enough to stimulate photosynthesis. If possible, move the plant to a sunnier window, or place it near reflective surfaces such as white or light-color walls. In extreme situations, you can even place mirrors, foil, or white backdrops about the plant.

Too much light causes plants to wilt and their vibrant green color to fade. Young, thin leaves are affected first because they cannot hold much water. Inexperienced indoor gardeners often miss this problem by attributing the symptoms to a lack of nutrients. Before you rush to fertilize a drooping plant, check its light requirements and how they are being met. Keep in mind that excessive light intensity is most likely to occur at midday. Some plants may even wilt slightly during this time and recover later in the day.

Another thought to keep in mind is that plants grow in the direction of the strongest light source. You may notice that after a period of time your plants appear to be "leaning" toward the window. They are actually growing toward the light and it is a good idea to rotate the plant occasionally so that it maintains a balanced shape.

Sunlight at Various Window Exposures

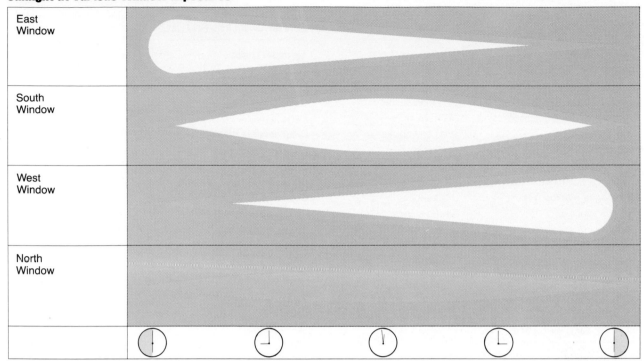

The duration and intensity of sunlight varies at different window exposures. A south-facing window receives the most intense sun for the longest period while a north-facing exposure receives only indirect light and for a short duration. Afternoon sun from the west is warmer than morning sun in an eastern window.

Light Categories

To establish some good general guidelines for assessing the light situations in your home and selecting plants to fit them, we can say that there are five basic light exposure categories for indoor plants:

Full Sun

Full sun describes locations that receive as much light as possible. These can be found within 2 feet of a south-facing window. This means at least 5 hours of direct sun. Very few plants other than cacti and some succulents will survive the heat in this setting in the summer; however, with some shade protection and plenty of water, many indoor plants that prefer bright sun will flourish here.

Some Direct Sun

Some direct sun refers to areas that are brightly lit but receive less than 5 hours of direct sun during the day. Window sills facing east or west and locations at least 2 feet but not much more away from a south-facing window usually fit this category. Some protection from intense summer sun is usually neces-

sary in west-facing windows. These locations are ideal for many flowering houseplants and some foliage houseplants.

Bright Indirect Light

Bright indirect light describes locations that receive as much light as possible without any direct sun. These can be found within 5 feet of a window that receives direct sun for part of the day only. Most foliage plants prefer this setting.

Partial Shade

Partial shade refers to locations that receive indirect light of varying intensity. They can be found in the zone between 5 to 8 feet from a window that receives direct sun part of the day. Areas near sunless windows can also fit this category. Few flowering plants, but a fair number of foliage plants, will adapt to this lighting.

Shade

Shade refers to poorly lit areas far from windows that receive direct sunlight. Only a few plants will tolerate such low light conditions.

Plants for each of these five categories are listed on page 14.

The graph on this page illustrates how light exposures can differ at different windows. These will help you visualize the definitions of the exposure categories. Use the categories and maps to determine the light level situations in your home. Once you have done this, you can check the optimum light recommendations in the "Gallery of Houseplants" (starting on page 55) to help you plan your indoor landscape, position any plants you now have, and select new ones.

There are many factors to consider in assessing light situations and each home has its own conditions. Keep in mind that the guidelines we have given you are of necessity only general ones, and while they will prove helpful, only you can determine from your own experience exactly where your houseplants will get the best light.

In this section we have been discussing natural light. Remember that artificial lighting can always make it possible to supplement light and grow plants in places that otherwise would be impossible. For information on artifical lighting, see page 38.

PLANTS FOR DIFFERENT LIGHT CATEGORIES

Botanical name	Common name	Botanical name	Common name
Plants for Full Sun		**Plants for Bright Indirect Light**	
Agave species	Agave	Adiantum species	Maidenhair fern
Allium schoenoprasum	Chives	Asplenium nedus	Bird's nest fern
Aloe species	Aloe	Brassaia actinophylla	Schefflera
Cephalocereus senilis	Old man cactus	Caladium species	Caladium
Chrysanthemum morifolium	Florist's mum	Caryota mitis	Fishtail palm
Echeveria species	Hen and chicks	Chamaedorea elegans	Parlor palm
Echinopsis species	Urchin cactus	Chamaerops humilis	European fan palm
Euphorbia pulcherrima	Poinsettia	Chlorophytum comosum	Spider plant
Gymnocalycium denadatum	Spider cactus	Chrysalidocarpus lutescens	Areca palm
Hydrangea macrophylla	Hydrangea	Codiaeum variegatum	Croton
Lithops species	Living stones	Coffea arabica	Coffee plant
Mammillaria species	Pincushion cactus	Columnea species	Columnea
Opuntia species	Opuntia	Davallia mariesii	Squirrel's foot fern
Pelargonium species	Geranium	Dieffenbachia species	Dieffenbachia
Rhipsalis species	Chain cactus	Dizygothica elegantissima	False aralia
Rosa hybrids	Miniature roses	Dracaena species	Dracaena
		Fatshedera	Aralia ivy
Plants for Some Direct Sun		Fatsia japonica	Japanese aralia
Abutilon species	Flowering maple	Ficus species	Ficus
Aechmea species	Living vase plant	Howea forsterana	Kentia palm
Aeschynanthus species	Lipstick plant	Orchids:	
Ananas species	Pineapple	Cattleya	
Aphelandra squarrosa	Zebra plant	Dendrobium	
Araucaria heterophylla	Norfolk Island pine	Oncydium	Dancing lady
Asparagus species	Asparagus fern	Paphiopedilum	Lady slipper
Azalea species	Azalea	Phalaenopsis	Moth orchid
Beaucarnea species	Bottle palm	Phoenix roebelenii	Pygmy date palm
Begonia species	Begonia	Pillaea rotundifolia	Button fern
Billbergia species	Vase plant	Platycerium bifurcatum	Staghorn fern
Blechnum gibbum	Lomaria	Polypodium aureum	Polypody fern
Camellia species	Camellia	Pteris cretica	Ribbon fern
Ceropegia woodii	Rosary vine	Rhapis excelsa	Large lady palm
Clivia miniata	Kaffir lily	Saintpaulia species	African violet
Coleus hybrids	Coleus	Streptocarpus species	Cape primrose
Crassula argentea	Jade plant		
Cryptanthus species	Earth stars	**Plants for Partial Shade**	
Cyclamen species	Cyclamen	Cissus species	
Episcia species	Episcia	Epipremnum aureum	Pothos; Devil's ivy
Faucaria species	Tiger's jaws	Philodendron bipinnatifidum	Twice-cut philodendron
Fuchsia hybrida	Fuchsia	Philodendron gloriosum	
Gardenia jasminoides	Gardenia	Philodendron hastatum	Spade-leaf philodendron
Hippeastrum species	Amaryllis	Philodendron oxycardium	Heart-leaf philodendron
Impatiens species	Impatiens	Philodendron 'Red Emerald'	
Kalanchoe species	Kalanchoe	Philodendron selloum	Lacy tree philodendron
Neorgelia species	Neoregelia	Spathiphyllum species	Peace lily; Spathe flower
Nephrolepis exaltata	Sword fern		
Primula species	Primrose	**Plants for Shade**	
Schlumbergera species	Christmas cactus	Aglaonema modestum	Chinese evergreen
Sedum morganianum	Donkey's tail	Aspidistra elatior	Cast-iron plant
Senecio rowleyanus	String-of-beads		
Sinningia speciosa	Gloxinia		
Vriesia species	Vriesia		

TEMPERATURE, HUMIDITY, AND AIR

All of the elements of a plant's environment must be in balance to ensure continuing health and growth.

Temperature

Temperature interacts with light, humidity, and air circulation to directly affect plant metabolism. Most plants we grow indoors adapt to the temperatures normally found in our homes, around 70°F days and 65°F nights. At night almost all plants benefit from at least a 5°F drop in temperature. This gives them a breather from the rapid rate of transpiration during the day, when temperatures are higher and water loss is greater. Overnight any water deficit in leaf cells is made up as roots take up water.

If you assume from the reading on your thermostat that your house or apartment temperature is uniform, you are likely to be in for a surprise. Generally variations occur even within each room. Use a thermometer to check the temperatures of different locations in your home and how they change in the course of the day.

Seasonal temperature changes must also be taken into account. Winter temperatures are particularly important to watch because they vary widely due to home heating and cold air that enters the house at windows and doors. Seasonal changes can be sudden and severe enough to warrant moving a plant to a new location, especially if it is growing on a window sill.

Tropical plants that are native where temperatures and humidity are high, such as episcias, fish-tail palms, and bougainvilleas, may do best near a south-facing window in a room with an appliance that vents moist heat, such as a dishwasher, a clothes dryer, or a humidifier.

Cool-loving plants (55 to 60°F days and 50°F nights) such as cyclamen, camellias, azaleas, and some orchids do well in rooms where indirect sun keeps temperatures low.

After a careful appraisal of your growing space, you will be able to select plants and locations compatible enough to produce good, vigorous growth.

A pebble tray filled with water to just below the tops of the rocks supplies humidity for maidenhair fern, pilea, and begonia. Below: Moist moss humidifies a peperomia plant.

Humidity

Humidity refers to the moisture content of the air. It is expressed as relative humidity: A percentage of the maximum amount of water vapor the air can hold at a given temperature.

Nearly all houseplants prefer a humidity level of 50 percent or higher; but in drier climates it is practically impossible to create this level of humidity in a home. As a result, many houseplants suffer from low humidity. This is especially true in winter, when dry home heating robs the air of moisture. At this time of year, humidities of 4 to 10 percent are common.

A cool vapor humidifier is one excellent way to increase the humidity in your home. Portable units can be placed wherever they are needed. Or, you may want to have a humidifier installed as a part of your home's central heating system. These units are relatively inexpensive and may be well worth the cost because humidified air is more comfortable for people as well as for plants. Such systems should have the capability of raising the humidity by 25 or 30 percent, even on the coldest winter days.

The simplest method for humidifying the air around plants is to set pots in trays or saucers filled with pebbles, perlite, or vermiculite. Fill these with enough water to reach just below the surface of the material, being careful not to add so much that the bottom of the pot touches the water (or else the roots may rot). As the water evaporates it fills the surrounding air with moisture. Just be sure to add water to the tray as it evaporates. Also, if plants are grouped together rather than separated, the leaves will catch and hold transpired moisture. Allow enough room between plants to allow some air circulation and discourage fungus disease from forming.

Misting, unless done several times a day, only temporarily raises the humidity around plants. If the room humidity is low, the moisture will evaporate quickly. Humidifying the air and keeping plants adequately watered are the only ways to ensure that they have sufficient moisture.

Air Circulation

Air circulation is as important to plants as it is to people. Just as you enjoy fresh air, it also helps plants to thrive. Soft breezes of warm humid air supply necessary oxygen and moisture. When plants are cramped together so that air cannot circulate among them, or are placed in an environment that lacks circulation, fungus disease is much more likely to occur.

The movement of dry air over leaves is another matter; this can cause moisture stress and leaf burn, especially in direct sun. Sudden changes in air movement and temperature do not benefit plants, either. These can send plants into *shock,* a state of decline brought about when chemical growth processes stall or stop due to radical environmental changes. Be careful if you keep your plants near a window, especially during winter, when cold drafts and frosted window panes can cause great harm.

Pollutants in the air can also harm plants. Fumes from burning propane or butane gas are likely to cause flowering plants to drop their buds. They can also cause leaves to yellow and drop off. Fumes from burning natural gas are not harmful to plants.

Dust and dirt can accumulate on houseplant leaves, clogging the stomata and slowing growth. A simple but highly effective way to keep plants clean is to place them in the shower once a month and give them a good rinse. Just be sure there is a removable screen in the drain to catch any soil or plant material that splashes from the pot. Between showers you can simply wipe off dust with a soft rag or feather duster, taking care not to harm the leaves.

Wipe dust off leaves with a damp cloth.

HOW TO BUY A HOUSEPLANT

An important key to a vigorous, long-lasting indoor garden is to start out with the healthiest plants you can find. Look at your purchase as an investment: Take the time to find out where you can get the best plants for your money, and most importantly, always examine them carefully before you buy. This way you'll get off to a good start and spare yourself much trouble in the long run.

Here are a few points to heed when buying plants:

- Watch for brown edges on leaves or evidence that they have been manicured away.
- Large gaps between new leaves suggest that heavy doses of fertilizer have been applied to induce rapid growth, or that the plants have been held too long in inadequate light.
- Inspect the leaves and the junctures of stems and leaves for any signs of insects or disease. This is most important, because if these problems sneak into your home on a new plant they can spread to your entire collection.
- Flowering plants should have lots of buds just ready to open. If they are already blooming, much of their beauty may already be spent.
- Check any supporting stakes or screens to make sure they aren't hiding broken stems, branches, or trunks.

Keeping these points in mind should help you select good, healthy houseplants—and save you from buying something that is pretty but impossible to keep alive.

GETTING STARTED

Initially a new plant will require more than a simple day-to-day care routine. Special tasks such as supplying good, nutrient-rich soil and repotting into suitable containers, or arranging plants in hanging baskets or terrariums, will have to be done early and with care to assure that your plants have the best chance at long-lasting health and beauty. The following pages explain how to do these special tasks and get your houseplants off to a good start in their new home.

Tools

Using the right tools will make your indoor gardening job much easier. To begin, find a solid surface to work on that you don't mind getting dirty, such as a piece of plywood or a table that's easy to clean. This is where you'll do your potting and grooming. It's a good idea to have several sizes of pots at hand and, for rooting cuttings or planting seeds, some plastic flats. Your soil needs should be met with a bag of all-purpose soil and, in addition, some soil amendments. (These are discussed later in this section.)

If you plan to take any cuttings, some powdered rooting hormone will be helpful. It's good to keep some liquid fertilizer handy as well, and a few broken pieces of clay pot will serve to cover drainage holes and keep soil from flowing out the bottoms of containers. You may have heard gravel recommended for this purpose and as a means of improving drainage and enhancing plant growth; however, experimentation has proved that gravel merely occupies space that otherwise could be filled with nutrient-rich soil.

Equip yourself with a good pair of pruning shears and a sharp knife for dividing plants and removing them from pots. Shears are available in several sizes, from the standard down to small needlenose shears for delicate work.

A watering can with a long spout obviously will be useful, and brushes, sponges, or soft rags will serve to clean off the dust and grime that collects on large leaves, clogging air passages and dulling their sheen.

To closely assess temperature conditions in your home, a thermometer that records both maximum and minimum temperatures will prove quite useful. Another instrument that can be quite valuable is a *hygrometer*, used to measure relative humidity.

Acclimating New Plants

When you bring a new plant home from the store it will need to adjust to its new surroundings. It may even go through a mild case of shock. In a very short time it has travelled from the meticulously controlled environment it enjoyed in the commercial greenhouse, to the retailer, and finally to a home with reduced light, lower humidity, and fluctuating temperatures.

This acclimation period will take a few weeks. In the first week leaves may yellow and blossoms may drop. During the acclimation period try to pay special attention to its needs. If you have chosen a plant that tolerates low light conditions, remember that it probably has been grown in strong light and needs time to adjust to the change in light intensity. If possible, make this change gradual by placing the plant in one or two interim locations with decreasing light intensity for at least a month in each spot. Finally, place the plant in the chosen site and give it a few weeks to begin actively growing again. If it doesn't grow or steadily declines, a brighter location may be the answer.

SOIL

All plant roots need water, air, and certain mineral nutrients. These are held in the minute spaces among soil particles. Nutrients dissolve in the water held in the smaller spaces, and water in larger spaces drains through the soil, leaving them filled with air.

For these reasons we say that soil should provide a plant with a root environment that is well draining (and thus well aerated) and yet retains enough moisture and nutrients for healthy growth.

Soil is made up of minerals, organic matter, and micro-organisms that convert organic matter into plant nutrients. The mineral portion

Mix homemade potting soil thoroughly. Place broken crockery over the drainage hole of the pot, gently fill in around the rootball with soil, and leave about one inch between the soil surface and the pot's rim.

of soil is classified by particle size into three types: In descending order of size they are sand, silt, and clay.

Soils with high proportions of sand, the largest particles, drain too freely to retain much moisture or nutrients. Plants in very sandy soils will have to be watered and fertilized too often to be practical. Soils high in silt hold nutrients and moisture better, but drain poorly. Soils high in clay, made up of the tiniest particles, are very rich in nutrients but have extremely poor drainage.

You can see that sand, silt, and clay all have desirable and undesirable characteristics. However, they can be blended in proportions that bring their advantages into play and cancel the disadvantages. Ideal soils are called *loam* soils, and they combine the capacity of silt and clay to hold nutrients and moisture with the good drainage and aeration of sand. (The proportions of loam range from: 23 to 53 percent sand, 28 to 50 percent silt, and 7 to 27 percent clay.)

The organic matter in soil serves many purposes. When broken down by micro-organisms it forms *humus*, the dark brown or black material that gives soil its distinctive color, provides nutrients, and enables the soil to form "crumbs" that best hold air, water, and nutrients.

Adding organic amendments such as peat moss, manure, ground bark, leaf mold, or compost will improve any soil. They will increase drainage and aeration in clay and silt soils (*heavy* soils); and will increase the moisture- and nutrient-holding ability of sandy soils.

Acidity and Alkalinity

Another important aspect of soil is its acidity or alkalinity. This is measured by the *pH* scale, which runs from 0 to 14, with 7 being neutral. A pH reading higher than 7 is on the alkaline side; a reading less than 7 is on the acid side.

Different plants have different pH preferences, but most plants we grow indoors prefer a slightly acid soil with a pH between 6.5 and 7. This is the range in which the major plant nutrients in the soil are most readily available. Most commercial potting soils and mixes you make yourself will be acidic because they contain organic matter whose components are acidic.

A highly alkaline soil will cause a plant to lose leaf color and will stunt its growth. Highly acid soil produces wilting and dropping leaves. If you have reason to believe pH is a problem with your plants, you can test the soil yourself with one of the inexpensive kits commonly available at garden centers.

Mixing Your Own Soil

Unless you have a place to prepare potting soils, time to do the work, and a source of ingredients, it's easier to buy ready-to-use soil. There are many brands available and some are far superior to others. Ask for recommendations from your local nursery or plant store. Make sure the soil is appropriate for your plant and that it's light enough to provide adequate drainage and root aeration. If prepackaged soils do not drain well, you can lighten them with organic amendments or with perlite, pumice, or vermiculite.

If you do mix your own soil, the following basic recipes should meet your needs. If you use soil from the garden you must sterilize it to eliminate harmful organisms, weed seeds, and pests. The process is easy: Merely place the soil in a covered container in the oven at 200°F. Insert a thermometer in the soil and keep its temperature between 150° and 180°F for 30 minutes. Baking the soil produces an unpleasant smell— so beware.

All-Purpose Mix

A good all-purpose potting mix can be made by combining 2 parts sterilized garden soil, 1 part leaf mold, and 1 part clean sand. Most people use common builder's sand—never use beach sand because it may contain salt, which will seriously harm plants. This mix will suit a great many plants. Soilless mixes (see below) are also excellent all-purpose mixes.

African Violet Mix

African violets, begonias, philodendrons, and azaleas grow well in a mixture that has a high humus content and is more acid. For these try equal parts sand, peat moss, sterilized garden soil, and leaf mold. You can buy this type of soil premixed; it is sold as African violet mix.

Cactus Mix

Plants from the desert need a growing medium that is gritty, neutral in pH, and low in organic matter. Most cacti and other succulents will prosper in a mixture of 1 part garden soil, 1 part sand, ½ part decayed leaf mold, and ½ part crushed clay flowerpot or brick. To each half bushel of this mixture, add a cup each of ground horticultural limestone and bone meal. This is sold as cactus mix in nurseries and garden centers.

Epiphytes, or *air plants*, derive most of their moisture and nutrients from the air and rain. They do not need soil and are cultivated in such mediums as osmunda fiber, unshredded sphagnum moss, and chipped redwood bark. Most orchids and bromeliads are classed as epiphytes.

Take advantage of soil substitutes. Horticultural perlite is as light as a feather and makes a good substitute for sand. Vermiculite, in place of leaf mold, will lighten and condition heavy, sticky soil and make it accceptable to plants that need a well-aerated medium. These inexpensive substitutes are already sterilized.

Mixing "Soilless Soils"

During the 1950s, container gardeners began using soilless growing mediums. These mixes do not contain any garden soil, whose composition can vary widely; instead, they consist of a careful blend of sterile organic material. Today, professional growers prefer these mixes because they can control their ingredients and thus control the way a plant will grow. Growers are even able to design blends especially suited to specific plant groups, such as African violets, bromeliads, and cacti.

The two most popular soilless mixes were developed at Cornell University and the University of California. The Cornell formula is available under such trade names as Jiffy Mix, Pro Mix, and Redi-Earth. The University of California formula is sold under the names First Step and Super Soil. If you need a large quantity of these, you can save money by mixing your own.

The two mixes are similar, with the main difference being that the Cornell mix uses vermiculite instead of the fine sand used in the California mix. Here are the recipes:
Cornell: 4 quarts #2 grade vermiculite.
California: 4 quarts fine sand designated as 30-270 sand. (These

Glazed pottery in whimsical shapes.

numbers refer to the screen sizes the sand can pass through. Fine sand will pass through a 30-mesh screen but will not pass through a 270-mesh screen.)
Both:
4 quarts shredded peat moss
1 level tablespoon
   superphosphate
2 tablespoons limestone
4 tablespoons aged dried cow
   manure or steamed bone meal
It's most convenient to do your mixing in a large plastic pail or trash can. Make sure that it's clean and dry before mixing. A tight-fitting lid will keep insects out and also allow you to keep the medium nicely moist later and ready for potting.

POTS AND CONTAINERS

The particular pots you choose to grow your plants in directly influence how well they grow, what kind of care you should give them, and how well they look once planted.

The standard clay pot is hard to beat because it is both functional and attractive. There are many shapes, but sizes generally range from 2 to 18 inches in diameter, and they have drainage holes in the bottoms. Usually you can buy saucers to match, although they may be sold separately.

The unglazed porous clay allows air and water to move through the

Baskets of all designs will accommodate pots.

Line wire baskets with moss before planting them.

wall of the pot, so before you plant in a clay pot, soak it in a pail or basin of water—preferably for several hours. Otherwise the dry clay will rob needed moisture from the soil and the roots of your new plant, and you'll have to water more often at first.

Take precautions against the moisture that seeps through the bottoms of clay saucers. In time it will mar wood and rot carpeting. A round of half-inch-thick cork cut to fit beneath the saucer will dissipate the water and plastic and glazed ceramic saucers are moisture proof.

Before you reuse clay pots, scrub them clean with a stiff brush and warm water. You can also run them through the dishwasher. Ideally, they should be sanitized by placing them in the oven at 180°F for 30 minutes, or by soaking in a 1:10 solution of household bleach and water.

Plastic Pots

Plastic pots have the distinct advantage of being lightweight. They are generally less expensive than clay and come in the same range of sizes. In addition, they are not porous as are clay pots and therefore retain water much longer. Plants in plastic containers do not need to be watered as often. Because air does not move through the walls of these pots, soil drainage must be excellent.

Glazed Pottery

Glazed pottery containers can be highly decorative, especially for indoor plants. Attractive planters can add a distinctive touch to almost any kind of decor. Many nurseries and garden centers now stock an array of sizes and designs in glazed containers, including pots and trays for bonsai that can also be used for other plants or for miniature landscapes.

If you select a container that does not have drainage holes, the best practice is to grow the plant in a slightly smaller clay or plastic pot that does, and simply slip this inside the more decorative container. To camouflage the edges of the planted pot, carpet the soil surface with florist's sheet moss, water-polished stones, or small shells.

Wooden Boxes or Planters

Planters made of rot-resistant red-wood or cypress are great-looking and also long-lasting containers. Unfortunately, the commercial product is seldom well constructed and all too often held together by metal banding that rusts quickly. A good solution is to build or have someone else build your own wooden planter boxes to fit your particular needs.

Woven Baskets

Woven baskets make great holders for plants, but all of them rot quickly if subjected to constant moisture. Planting in them directly is unwise, and when using them purely for show, to hide a more utilitarian pot, be sure to include a saucer inside to collect water.

These richly colored, highly decorative Indian baskets complement, rather than detract from, the delicate maidenhair fern, bird's nest fern, and mosses.

POTTING TECHNIQUES

Plants need repotting when they are growing in extremely light shipping soil that requires constant watering and when they become potbound—that is, when they grow too many roots for their containers.

To lower shipping costs, growers often transport plants to nurseries in soil largely composed of ultralight vermiculite or perlite. This soil is fine for plants in the short run, but it quickly exhausts its limited supply of nutrients and will require frequent fertilizing. In addition, it is so porous that it dries out quickly and will demand more frequent watering. After you bring your plant home from the shop, give it a few days to a week to partially recover from the shock of shipping and changing environments; then, if the soil needs constant watering, repot it.

In time the roots gradually absorb all the minerals from the soil and form a tightly packed mass that inhibits growth. Repotting is essential when a plant outgrows its pot. To see if the roots are compacted, turn the plant on its side and knock the rim of the pot gently against a solid surface to loosen the rootball. (If it doesn't come out, the soil may be too wet.) If the roots are massed along the sides of the pot and at the base of the rootball, repot the plant.

In most instances it's advisable to move a plant up to a pot not more than 2 inches wider at the rim. A pot that is much larger gives the roots a large space to grow into. The top of the plant will not start to grow well until the roots begin to fill the container. In addition, if you put a plant into a large container, you'll just be feeding and watering a lot of extra soil.

A good general rule about pot size is to use a pot whose diameter at the top of the rim equals ⅓ to ½ the height of the plant. However, the rule does not hold for very tall, slender plants. These will grow well in smaller pots.

Hanging plants create dazzling window displays. The spider plant and Boston fern filter the bright light pouring into the room behind.

PLANTING HANGING BASKETS

Hanging containers allow you to get the most from the indoor gardening space you have. These are the aerialists of the plant world; they are at their best dangling or climbing—from beams, windows, above kitchen sinks, in corners, skylights, or down stairwells.

You can use pottery, wooden, wire, or plastic hanging baskets, commonly available at stores, or adapt regular clay and plastic flowerpots to the purpose. You can buy all kinds of decorative hangers—twine, string, leather, wire, or chain—or make your own from materials found in hobby shops. These can also hold a saucer in place to prevent water from dripping onto the floor.

It's a good idea to line wooden baskets with thick plastic or aluminum foil so that soil won't wash through cracks. Wire baskets (and plastic baskets with spaces between the ribs) need to be lined with coarse, unmilled sphagnum moss or sheet moss before filling with soil. Some growers go one step further and include an additional lining of burlap or a saucer to prevent soil from leaking.

The care of plants in hanging baskets is generally the same as for identical plants grown in any container. The most effective way to water hanging baskets thoroughly is to immerse them in a sinkful or pail of water. Allow the planting to soak, then drain it sufficiently so that the basket will not drip when it is rehung. Moss baskets should always be watered by this method to ensure thorough wetting.

TERRARIUMS

When you place several different plants in one container you can create a miniature landscape effect. This is true whether you are working with a shallow cast-iron or ceramic bonsai tray or making a terrarium with a fish tank, bubble bowl, brandy snifter, or bottle.

Depending upon your personal likes, the plants you have available, the container, and where you want your landscape to grow, you can create the effect of a woodland dell, the desert, a rocky or sandy coastline, or any landscape you find attractive.

If there is space in your terrarium you can add a shallow container of water to serve as a pond. Sometimes a small mirror is used to represent water, but the real thing is better, especially when creeping plants like baby tears grow around the "banks."

The most common misconception about terrariums is that they require no care and will thrive just about anywhere in your home. Don't be misled—they may not need the at-

Top: Maidenhair fern, bird's nest fern, and ivy. Below: African violets, parlor palm, and maidenhair fern.

tention required for most houseplants, but they do require some care. They need water from time to time and routine maintenance to remove spent growth and keep rampant growers compact. For these reasons, buying a preplanted terrarium that appears to be stuffed with plants is not a good investment: It will soon be overgrown.

Airborne Terrariums

Terrariums are more often thought of as tabletop decorations, but they can also be suspended from ceiling hooks or wall brackets. Almost any terrarium can be suspended, but there are leaded glass ones available that are especially designed for hanging.

A good point to remember when you set out to make a terrarium or bottle planting is that plants will do best if the glass you choose is clear, not tinted.

BOTTLE PLANTING

Bowls, dishes, brandy snifters, and fish tanks are easy to plant and maintain because you can reach inside with your hands. Small-neck bottles, on the other hand, are quite a challenge. You will find yourself expecting to use your hands to plant when you actually have to use long-handled tools.

To place your growing medium in the bottle, fashion a funnel from a rolled piece of newspaper. This will help keep particles of soil off the inside walls. To move the soil around and shape the terrain, you can use a piece of slender bamboo stake with a half-teaspoon measuring spoon taped to the end.

Before you add any plant to a bottle, inspect it carefully to be sure it has no insects or disease and that no roots are rotted. When you are ready to "bottle" your plants, gently remove most of the soil from the roots. Then drop each plant through the neck and, using your bamboo-spoon-spade, coax it into the right position and cover the roots with soil.

After the plants are in place, a final mulch or ground carpeting of green woods moss or florist's sheet moss will complete the scene. Use a mister of clear water to settle the roots and remove soil particles from the leaves and sides of the bottle. Be careful not to add too much water, or you'll have a floating garden.

Bottle gardens do best in bright indirect light. Sun shining directly on the bottle for more than an hour or two is likely to steam-cook the plants. They also do well under two fluorescent tubes—one cool white, one warm white, either 20 or 40 watts—for 12 to 14 hours each day.

If the soil appears dry, if no moisture droplets form inside, or if the plants appear lackluster and droopy, add a little water. To remove yellowing leaves, spent flowers, or excess growth, tape a single-edge razor blade to a piece of slender bamboo and use it as a cutting tool. You can remove clippings with 2 sticks of bamboo used chopstick fashion or with a mechanic's pick-up tool (sold at auto supply houses). It is important to remove dying leaves and flowers before they can rot. Once rot gets started, it may move quickly to healthy leaves and shoots.

Planting Terrariums

Most containers used for terrarium gardening have no drainage holes. To keep the growing medium sweet-smelling and conducive to healthy growth, line the bottom of the container with a half-inch of charcoal chips. You'll find these in bags wherever indoor plants and supplies are sold. Next add a minimum of 1½ inches of potting soil. It's easiest to use a commercially prepared medium specified for terrariums. The most common complaint with these is that they are too moisture retentive. If necessary, add some sand or perlite. Any of the soilless mixtures (see page 18) are fine for miniature landscapes.

For an intriguing display, grow a plant inside a clear glass bottle. The warm, humid atmosphere permits strong growth. Here we show an ivy growing up a piece of bark. Protect bottle plantings from prolonged direct sunlight; the glass magnifies the sun's heat.

CREATING THE INDOOR LANDSCAPE

Displaying houseplants to their best advantage ❧ Questions to ask yourself before arranging your plants ❧ Ideas for greenery in each room of your home

Indoor landscapes are as varied as the individuals who create them. Some people grow only a few plants and spread them throughout the house; others prefer a busy and vibrant atmosphere featuring groups of many different plants in all shapes and sizes. One gardener may blend foliage and flowering plants to create a splash of color against a backdrop of green. And then there's the plant collector who concentrates on growing one type of plant, such as cacti or orchids, and designs around it.

In all cases, what makes indoor gardens work both functionally and aesthetically is the forethought and planning that goes into them.

In the following pages we raise some basic design questions to keep in mind when selecting and arranging your houseplants. The accompanying photos, design concepts, ideas, and plant lists will arm you with loads of practical suggestions for arranging your plants to bring out their best features, and enhance the beauty of your home.

Remember, there are no absolutes in designing with houseplants. New styles constantly evolve into still newer styles, and old styles are revived. We can give you good, sound principles, but creating an indoor landscape remains a highly individual task: The more creative you are, the more distinctive your indoor garden will be.

Fishtail palms, Norfolk Island pines, and maidenhair ferns enliven this office setting.

BASIC CONSIDERATIONS

As you set out to create your own individual indoor landscape, ask yourself the questions that follow; they'll familiarize you with some basic design considerations. The way you answer them will help you determine what plants to select and how best to use their individual features to complete your design. Keeping these questions in mind will make the difference between your having a haphazard jumble of houseplants or a beautiful, balanced collection that makes your home even lovelier.

What is the environment in the room in which you want to grow plants; how does it meet the cultural requirements of your houseplants?

Although this question may not appear to concern design, it overrides every other consideration. A sickly plant is unsightly wherever it grows, however it is used.

Take note of the temperature, humidity, and light conditions in your home and try to choose only plants that thrive in those conditions. Keep cultural factors foremost in your design thoughts. Refer to the "Gallery of Houseplants" (pages 55 to 93) for the environmental and care requirements of the individual plants you want to grow.

How healthy and attractive your houseplants are also depends on how much time you can spend caring for them. In general, flowering plants need more grooming than

foliage specimens. For detailed information on caring for plants, see pages 35 to 45.

What are the structural confines in the rooms you want to decorate with plants?

Survey a room's overall dimensions, the locations of windows, the placement of heating and cooling ducts, the furniture arrangement, traffic patterns, wasted or empty space, color, and design scheme. Note where plants will fit comfortably in the room design or improve its appearance.

What is the scale and shape of the plant in relation to the scale of the room?

A large, branching fiddleleaf fig will overpower a small sitting room; a single fern or prayer plant will go unnoticed in the corner of a large, open interior. Generally, a large plant looks most appropriate placed in a room spacious enough to balance its size. A small plant, on the other hand, is best displayed in a spot where its delicate features can be seen and appreciated.

Will each plant or group of plants create a focal point within a room?

Displayed in a decorative hanging basket, the arching leaves and shoots of a large spider plant will attract attention to a dull corner at the far end of a room. The same plant tucked into a corner near an entryway would be missed by most. As you would with your best

Careful selection and placement of plants instill this bright living room with a fresh, relaxing atmosphere. The weeping fig next to the corner window thrives, and draws a connection between nature indoors and out. Azaleas and forced narcissus create a pool of color in the center of the room. The row of dracaena on the left acts as a room divider, separating the study area from the sitting area.

pieces of furniture, display your houseplants where they will add the most to the total decorating scheme. Make sure also that the location you choose for a plant has sufficient space to accommodate it, so it won't look cramped as it grows. Place plants in settings that capitalize on their distinctive shapes to advance the room's theme or style.

Will the plant blend well with other plants in the room?

A massive collection of different types of plants accumulated randomly can easily make for a cluttered, ineffective display. A well-planned grouping, however, can be compelling and impressive. Choose plants that are compatible culturally and work together aesthetically to create dynamic, unified compositions.

Does the leaf shape and plant form complement the decor of the room?

Certain plants look better than others when combined with the particular design features of a room. Almost all plants look best with an undecorated wall for a background. Bright or large-leaf foliage provides a nice contrast to small, delicate wallpaper and fabric patterns. Boldness of form and leaf pattern enhance design schemes with neutral tones and solid colors.

Will the colors of the plant blend with, add to, or compete with the color of the room?

Use flowering plants to pick up the hues present in the furnishings and walls. The shapes of the blooms can reflect and accent the patterns in wallpapers and upholstery, especially if they feature a flower design.

How will the plant supports and containers blend with the interior furnishings?

Containers are important to a plant display: Choose them carefully to enhance the plant's appearance and its compatibility with the design of the room. For example, a ceramic American Indian pot makes a nice home for a cactus in an adobe style house, but the same pot planted with a delicate fern might look awkward.

How will lighting enhance the appearance of a plant in a particular setting?

Spotlights can make a display much more striking, especially for plants in dark or out-of-the-way settings. Hanging plants spotlighted in a large entryway will catch the eye immediately, especially at night. Lights placed beneath large-leaf plants will project dramatic shadows on ceilings and walls behind the plants. For more about lighting, see page 38.

Fishtail palm and Swedish ivy, on the floor, add to the exotic appeal of the decorative furniture. Flaming red amaryllis plants form the focal point while a mother-in-law's tongue and cuttings of a piggyback plant flank the striking blooms with green. Opposite: A weeping fig with ivy growing at its base and blooming cape primroses fill the bright, open space below a spiral stairway.

SOLVING DESIGN PROBLEMS WITH HOUSEPLANTS

Striking foliage and blossoming flowers make useful, relatively inexpensive architectural tools. They create divisions, add color, alter scale, fill empty spaces, and obscure architectural defects within a room. A plant can be found for almost any purpose.

Plants as Room Dividers

Many homes feature large open interiors. Although you may enjoy their sense of spaciousness, undoubtedly there are times when you wish you had the divisions and privacy that walls and partitions provide.

With an effective arrangement of plants you can achieve separation without totally obliterating the open-air atmosphere. Mass together several medium or large plants such as croton, coffee plant, schefflera, or podocarpus. Or perhaps a free-standing weeping fig tree or palm will be enough to block the view and divide the area.

Trained on wooden trellises, stakes, or canes, such plants as philodendron, creeping fig, or grape ivy will build a wall of green between two areas. For a more subtle trellis division, construct a string or wire trellis. Just place tacks in the plant container or the floor and in the ceiling. Attach wire or string in whatever pattern you desire and train the plants to grow up the framework.

Hanging baskets also can divide space. Suspend 2 or 3 from strong ceiling hooks. Columneas, grape ivies, or spider plants make nice hanging displays.

In a small house or apartment the front door often opens right into the living room. A planter box will help create an entrance area, and also will serve as a natural welcome for your guests.

A two-sided bookcase also makes an attractive and functional room divider and plant setting. Install one in a kitchen that opens into a dining area or in a television room with an area set aside for reading. Intersperse plants with books and other items at different levels throughout the shelves. If the room is not well lit you may want

to install some artificial lighting for some of the shelves. Otherwise just grow some shade-loving plants such as the small-leaf wandering Jew, perhaps contrasted with the bold, quilted leaves of creeping Charlie. If you already have a room divider or screen, soften the divider lines and create a continuity between the rooms by training a small-leaf ivy to drape over its top.

Plants to Fill Empty and Dark Spaces

How many times have you looked around your house wondering how you could make empty dull corners, blank walls, and unused areas disappear, or better yet, transform them into attractive features? Plants are a relatively easy and inexpensive solution to the problem.

These spots are perfect havens for shade-tolerant plants. Use palms, dracaenas, sansevieria, schefflera, monsteras, or philodendrons. Despite their shade tolerance, supplemental artificial light will noticeably enhance their performance. Spotlight the group at night for an exciting display or add a little color by incorporating flowering plants in season.

Stairways are often veritable reservoirs of wasted vertical space. Enliven them by trailing plants from wall brackets or line pots of trailing plants along the stairs. For large plain stairway walls attach a wooden or metal lattice to a wall and run philodendrons or arrowhead vine up it. Many townhouses, condominiums, and bi-level homes feature open slatted stairways. The somewhat isolated area under an open stairway can be used to grow a group of plants such as cast-iron plants, false aralias, ferns, Chinese evergreens, nerve plants, and pileas.

Untrafficked, unusable pools of space often form around furniture arrangements. Instead of rearranging the furniture, use the space to create a natural composition by arranging several plants on stands of various levels, or simply focus the arrangement on a large branching tree; try a fiddleleaf fig or fishtail palm.

Plants as Camouflage

Plants can disguise certain architectural obstructions, converting them into striking natural design features. For instance, when faced with a bothersome pillar or pole in the midst of a room, instead of trying to ignore it and steering guests around it, use plants to soften its lines and make it blend into the room. Encircle the base with a mass of plants or train vines to grow all around it.

Another example is found in the big unsightly radiators that haunt many owners and decorators of older homes. With a few simple adjustments and some conscientious plant care, radiators become surprisingly nice plant settings. A board and some bricks are all you really need to construct a buffer zone between the hot radiator and plant tray. The buffer will dissipate the heat and moderate the temperature changes so that plants will grow. Nevertheless, it's best to select tolerant plants that prefer dry warm conditions. Cacti and succulents are a good choice. Podocarpus, lipstick plant, pothos, geraniums, and kalanchoe may also work, depending on how much light is available. Deep humidifying trays

are a necessity for anything other than cacti and succulents in these conditions; they should always be kept filled with water. One lapse in your care routine could prove fatal.

Having an empty fireplace as a feature in a room is not uncommon, but certainly not necessary. At first it may appear an unlikely, almost forbidding place to grow plants; but plants arranged in front of the opening will enliven the fireplace with flames of greenery. Boston ferns or cast-iron plants, for example, will do well next to the secluded, somewhat damp confines of a fireplace. Block off the chimney before you arrange the plants; otherwise the space will be drafty and the plants will suffer. For further decoration around the fireplace, flank each side with rubber trees or palms. Smaller fireplaces can be decorated with mature jade plants displayed in floor baskets.

Protruding corners caused by closets or recessed areas are unsightly as well as hazardous for people who forget to watch where they walk. Ferns, piggybacks, creeping Charlie, and Swedish ivy hung at various levels with wall brackets will hide and soften the corner.

A Chinese evergreen, kentia palm, and a centerpiece of African violets enhance the elegance of this dining room. Opposite: Grace a dark fireplace with shade tolerant plants. Chinese evergreen, ivy, peace lily, and mother-in-law's tongue decorate the floor while another peace lily and a dancing lady orchid add flair in the brighter light on the mantelpiece.

This formal living room features, clockwise, a peace lily, cyclamen, African violets, kentia palm, and Chinese evergreen. The peace lily and Chinese evergreen grow well in the lower light their positions afford.

PLANT ARRANGEMENTS ROOM BY ROOM

Some plants look more appropriate in certain rooms than others. For instance, tomato vines hanging in a kitchen or informal dining room look fine; in a living room they look out of place. In addition some rooms such as bathrooms, porches, and utility rooms are typically humid and either very bright or very shady, making them hospitable to only a few specific plants. The following suggestions feature plants that will advance the theme or purpose of a room, or take advantage of its particular cultural conditions. For more design ideas for different decors and settings see the section, "Blending Plants Into Your Interior Design", page 32.

Living Rooms and Dining Rooms

Flowering plants instill living rooms and dining rooms with grace and elegance. Bay windows (often found in these two rooms) lined with blooming impatiens, gloxinias, cape primrose, kalanchoe, forced bulbs, or chrysanthemums look stunning no matter what style the interior.

Coordinate the colors of the blossoms with the colors in the room.

You can create the same kind of arrangement in front of large windows or unused sliding glass doors. Place the plants on the floor or on an unobtrusive plant stand. For a less linear, ordered appearance, arrange the pots on clear plastic tubular stands of different heights; they will allow light to reach all the plants.

In the dining room, accent the colors in tableware and upholstery fabrics with groups of colorful blooms grown in corners or near windows; or draw the outdoor garden colors seen through windows into the indoors by placing a white wicker basket plant stand with similar flowering plants next to the windows. For a simple decoration use a houseplant as a table centerpiece; try cape primrose, lilies, wax begonias, azaleas, orchids, or forced bulbs.

Kitchens

Kitchens are practical, busy homemaking environments—and usually a favorite spot in the house. Evoke the feeling of abundance and add a country air with the flourishing beauty of geraniums. Grow them in the breakfast nook or place them by the window, perhaps above the

sink. Advance the theme of food directly by growing some of your own right inside the house. Container varieties of tomatoes grow

Clockwise: Cyclamen, amaryllis, Boston fern, pothos, and piggyback plants.

well in particularly bright windows and add a lovely red and green composition to the room. (See Ortho's *All About Tomatoes* for more indoor growing information.) Herbs, chives, and garlic will grow under fluorescent lights or on a sunny countertop and will come in handy while cooking.

Another alternative is to install a window box outside a kitchen window to grow herbs or flowers. Inside the window you can grow plants similar in color or complementary in size. This will add depth to your indoor garden without using up any more space. Also don't forget to coordinate your plants with the color and design of wallpaper, cabinets, counters, and table settings.

Porches and Enclosed Patios

Glass or screen enclosed porches or patios are unique, spectacular settings for many plants that love the sun and can tolerate the erratic temperatures commonly found in these unheated areas. On chilly nights you may have to protect your plants by covering them or bringing them inside. A host of plants, both large and small, can be grown depending on the look you wish. Large porches are good spots for plant collections. Install shelves to display and organize them. Hardy vines trained up the sides of roof supports of porches are very attractive and lend a warm look to the area. Blooming clivias lining the sides of a glass enclosed entryway or porch look striking. Pots of calla lilies appear equally as exotic and colorful.

Bedrooms and Bathrooms

Plants grown in the bedroom will make it an even more pleasant place to be. Waking to flowering plants and live greenery is sure to help you ease into your daily routine. Choose your personal favorites. The bedroom also presents the chance to watch closely the progress of a plant. Grow a pot of flowering forced bulbs at the window next to your bed. Each morning you can observe the fascinating development that occurred through the night.

Children's bedrooms and play-

rooms present the opportunity to use plants as a learning tool. Arrange a collection of tolerant plants with particularly interesting growth habits. Piggyback plant, spider plant, sensitive plant, baby's tears, rosary vine, peperomias, and succulents are among the best.

Offices

Offices once seemed unlikely homes for plants, but that time has passed. Today, many offices with plants in their midst exude a refreshing vitality. People who work in the presence of plants tend to find the environment more hospitable. Just the simple addition of an African violet or another small plant on a desk top can improve the atmosphere.

Offices generally are designed purely from a functional perspective, and the harsh lines that can result are softened by the addition of a little greenery. Hardy plants such as cast-iron plant, Japanese fatsia, or jade plant should do well, but with adequate light you can grow any houseplant. If you grow plants with high light requirements, keep a fluorescent light at the proper distance from them and leave it on after you leave the office, with a timer set to automatically turn the light off.

Top: Delicate touches of color—a weeping fig, a maidenhair fern, primroses, and cattails complement the artwork and fabrics in this bedroom. Above: A modern office exudes a fresh vitality with hanging ivies, ferns, philodendrons, and weeping fig trees.

BLENDING PLANTS INTO YOUR INTERIOR DESIGN

Interior designs and decorating styles vary almost as much as the many thousands of different plants we bring indoors. In a room, a handful of basic design elements—wall coverings, furniture, ornamental decorations, and the room's layout—combine to create the style of the room, whether it's modern, western, provincial, Victorian, Mediterranean, or Early American. To help plants advance the theme consider how they blend with the predominant elements in the settings you have selected.

Modern Decor

Linear, unpatterned modern interiors become warm and comfortable with healthy green plants in their midst. Graceful palms and branching fig trees with their flowing branches, vibrant greenery, and exotic leaf shapes inject the atmosphere with a natural vitality and calmness unachievable by the architectural decorating scheme alone.

A butcherblock plant arrangement creates a natural division between kitchen and living room. Right: Clockwise, fiddle-leaf fig, zebra plant, umbrella tree, Boston fern, and an orchid add to the room's tropical feeling.

Traditional Interiors

Many Victorian and Early American homes look attractive with displays of ferns or palms. Large ferns placed on traditional-motif plant stands go well with the ornately carved antiques commonly found in these homes. A room furnished with provincial pieces takes on an even more antique flavor with the complement of ferns placed on natural wood stands. Placed on a more contemporary decorative plant stand they would detract from the simple elegance of the interior.

Adobe interior designs with natural colorings, tile flooring, and large windows are suitable decors for many plants. Bromeliads, cacti, and succulents—with their striking texture, color, and form—are the most fitting. The more refined Mediterranean interiors will also benefit from the addition of houseplants. The fine features of dracaena, its stark stems and burst of pointed foliage at the tips, mix well with the color and form of patterned upholstery and terrazzo flooring commonly found in this style interior.

Size of Plant Displays

Coordinating the size and scale of a plant display is a key factor in making it an attractive focal point within an interior. Placed in a room of the wrong size or scale, any plant display can be visually overbearing or lost.

Small rooms usually look best with a few small plants. You might want to hang a wandering Jew in an alcove, grow a mature jade plant in a floor basket, and place a podocarpus in a corner. These plants won't cramp the limited space and in fact their flowing branches might provide a visual relief from the compactness of the room. For a subtle touch of color, try growing a cape primrose, gloxinia, or African violet on a window sill, dresser, or coffee table. Some larger plants to grow in smaller rooms include bamboo palms and false aralias. These plants are delicate and subtle. They do not branch widely, but rather grow vertically, and therefore consume very little of the precious living space.

Above: Entryhall plants bloom in succession for nonstop color: florist's mum, amaryllis, and, finally, paper-white narcissus.

Below: Rubber trees, mistletoe fig, zebra plant, and croton make a stunning orderly display in this contemporary setting.

Large rooms are far more suitable for the bigger plants, such as ficus trees, monsteras, palms, and large orchids, and for big group displays of medium and small plants.

Small plants displayed alone tend to be lost in the spaciousness of the environment, but one way to offset this is to run a plant theme throughout a room by sprinkling several different variations of color or form of one plant throughout a room. Other small and medium-size specimens in large rooms will be more noticeable when displayed in decorative containers appropriate to the room design.

For more ideas and help with planning your design, study photographs in home decorating magazines and books. Watch for effective displays in other homes and in offices and stores. Consult a knowledgeable plant dealer—he or she will be able to help you choose the plants that work best in your particular environment. Then take all of this information and modify it to meet your own decorating needs.

DAY-TO-DAY CARE

Watering techniques ❧ Fertilizing methods ❧ Grooming your plants ❧
Artificial lighting ❧ Moving indoor plants outdoors and outdoor plants indoors

Houseplants are container plants, and the single most important concept to remember about container gardening is this: The roots of the plant are confined to the container; they cannot search deeper or wider for sustenance; therefore, the plant depends totally on you for nourishment and care.

HOW AND WHEN TO WATER

More houseplants die from improper watering than any other cause, and overwatering is the culprit more often than underwatering. Too much water coupled with poor drainage forces roots to sit in water, suffocate, and rot. When roots are unable to carry enough necessary oxygen to the rest of the plant, the result is wilt and decline. To avoid this problem, don't assume immediately that your plant needs water when it doesn't grow as you had expected. Your good intentions will be harmful if the plant is suffering from some other ailment.

Water needs are related to several factors. Individual species have specific preferences dictated long ago in their natural habitats. The light, temperature, and humidity you provide your plants will further affect and change moisture needs. How much moisture a plant uses also depends on the size and type

The umbrella tree and many other plants benefit from an occasional trip to the shower to clean the leaves and thoroughly soak the soil.

Check soil moisture by the touch test.

of container it grows in; if the pot is small, moisture will be absorbed quickly and the plant will have to be watered often. If you can't keep a plant moist, even if you water every day, then it needs repotting. Water needs are also determined by the plant's growth cycle. During active growth periods a plant will absorb more water than during its rest periods.

Your job is to learn exactly when your plant needs water. The simplest and most reliable way to tell is to insert your finger into the soil and test by touch; you'll be able to feel the degree of moisture. To double-check, rub a bit of the soil between your thumb and index finger. With a little experience you'll be able to tell into which of the following 3 general moisture categories your soil fits.

■ Evenly moist soil: This soil is moist throughout, but not so wet as to be soggy. The soil just below the surface will get your finger damp, but not muddy. The soil surface should never dry out completely or the plants will suffer. Ferns, gardenias, and African violets grow well at this moisture level.

■ Slightly damp soil: This soil is dry on the surface, with low moisture just below the surface. The soil is cool and damp to the touch but will not get your finger wet. Coleus, monstera, and philodendrons are among plants that prefer this level.

■ Moderately dry soil: This soil feels dry to the touch. It is dry below the surface to a depth of an inch; any deeper, and it's time to water. Peperomia, dieffenbachia, dracaena, and geraniums thrive in this soil moisture level.

When you've determined the moisture level of a plant's soil, you can compare it with the optimum level for that plant as recommended in the "Gallery of Houseplants," starting on page 55. This will give you a good idea when to water. Always water thoroughly. Gradually the soil will dry until it reaches a low moisture level and needs to be watered again. Every plant needs a thorough soak; it's the frequency of watering that varies.

Water each plant until the soil is saturated. The water should take a minute or two to drain; if it drains through very rapidly it may be just running down between the rootball and the pot and not soaking into all of the rootball. If your plant doesn't receive thorough soakings, but only superficial waterings, its roots will grow toward the surface of the soil.

Thorough watering will also help wash out accumulated fertilizer salts, which can build up and harm the plant. This buildup can be caused by overfertilizing and by watering too little to drain the salts. It is recognizable by a whitish deposit on the outside of clay pots or by salt burn on the edges of leaves. The condition is a serious one but can be remedied by watering through, or *leaching*, the soil thoroughly. Place the plant in a sink, tub, or pail and water it several times, each time letting the water drain. If salts have become a problem they will not leach out in one day; the process may have to be repeated weekly for several weeks.

Leach the soil outdoors with a hose to wash away harmful salt build-up accumulated from fertilizers and water.

It is easier and faster to water container plants from above, but submerging a pot in water up to its rim is excellent for plants you've allowed to dry out completely and for those that are in full bloom. Leave the pot submerged for several minutes after the air stops bubbling up. This is always the best way to water hanging plants or plants growing on slabs of tree fern. Drain the plant thoroughly before returning it to its growing space. Do not let the plant drain into the saucer and then sit in this water; pour the water off within an hour.

Water temperature is important. Tropical plants are the most sensitive, but all plants can be harmed by having cold water applied either to the roots or to the foliage. Always use tepid water. An occasional trip to the family shower rinses dust and dirt from the leaves and is an excellent way to water the plant thoroughly. Again, use tepid water.

Water softeners that replace the calcium in water with sodium produce water that will harm plants. Sodium accumulates in soil and does not settle out or evaporate. If you have a water softener, use a tap that is outdoors or install a tap in the water line before it goes into the softener so you'll have a source of unsoftened water for plants.

Alkaline Water

In parts of the country where soil is very alkaline and the water is very hard (that is, it contains a heavy concentration of minerals), it is difficult to grow acid-loving plants such as camellias and azaleas. Adding peat moss or other acid soil amendments to the soil and using fertilizers that have an acid reaction will help. In alkaline conditions plants cannot use trace minerals and iron. They will therefore benefit from regular applications of an iron chelate to keep the foliage a healthy green color. (Iron chelate is available at nurseries and garden centers, sometimes in formulations that contain added trace minerals.) When the new foliage on these plants is yellow, water with a solution of 1 ounce iron sulfate in 2 gallons of water. Repeat this every 2 weeks until growth regains a normal color.

HOW AND WHEN TO FERTILIZE

Nitrogen, phosphorus, and potassium are the three major nutrients needed by plants. When you pick up a container of houseplant fertilizer at your garden store, you'll see 3 numbers on the label. These are, in order, the percentages of nitrogen, phosphorus, and potassium. For example, a fertilizer labeled 12-6-6 is made up of 12 percent nitrogen, 6 percent phosphate, and 6 percent potash. Fertilizers come in many different formulations; for example, those designed for flowering plants usually contain less nitrogen than phosphorus and potassium, because nitrogen encourages foliage growth but at some expense of flowering.

In addition to foliage growth, nitrogen contributes to the deep green color of plants and to stem growth. Phosphorus encourages bloom and root growth, and potassium contributes to stem strength and disease resistance. In addition to these *primary nutrients*, plants need 3 *secondary nutrients*—sulfur, calcium, and magnesium—and minute quantities of iron, zinc, manganese, copper, chlorine, boron, and molybdenum. The latter are called *micronutrients*, or *trace minerals*.

As well as being manufactured in many formulations, fertilizers are available in many forms: water soluble pellets, powders, liquids, dry tablets and sticks to insert in the soil, and time-release pellets. The variety can be confusing, and value does vary widely. Any reliable plant seller will help you choose the best fertilizer for your needs.

In applying fertilizers, always read the label first and follow the directions carefully. Don't succumb to the notion that more is better. It takes only a little extra fertilizer to burn a plant's roots or leaves.

Container plants need regular feeding only when they are in active growth. Dormant or sick plants *never* benefit from the addition of fertilizers. Dormant plants are in a natural state of arrested growth and fertilizer is not needed. Wilting, yellowing, pallid plants that are suffering from something other than lack of fertilizer will decline even more rapidly if you feed them.

Brown leaf tips signal fertilizer burn.

These plants are in a state of shock and may even die if fed.

Before turning to fertilizers, review the care requirements of the plant and determine whether you have been meeting them properly. If you have been fertilizing regularly and the plant isn't growing, it's likely that the plant is dormant or sick.

Most houseplant fertilizers on the market have been formulated for use every 2 weeks. This is more effective and safer than large monthly doses. If monthly doses are recommended you can feed half the suggested amount every 2 weeks.

Too much fertilizer causes leaf tips and edges to turn brown in otherwise good growing conditions. Note the spider plant in the photograph on this page. Excess fertilizer also can cause premature dropping of the lower leaves and wilting of the entire plant. If you mistakenly overfeed a plant, leach out the fertilizer by applying copious amounts of water. Allow the soil to drain, then pour on more water. As a last resort, you can wash the old soil from the roots and repot into fresh new soil.

Foliar Feeding
In their native habitats, plants can absorb nitrogen and other nutrients from rain and bird droppings that fall onto their leaves. Fertilizers recommended for foliar application are available at garden stores. Apply these with a sprayer or mister every 2 to 4 weeks, following the label directions. Foliar feeding is quick-acting, lasts a relatively short time, and is best used as a supplement to a liquid fertilizer applied directly to the soil.

For a complete discussion of fertilizers, see the Ortho book, *Fertilizers, Soils & Water.*

GOOD GROOMING TECHNIQUES
Plants in containers need regular pruning and trimming to keep them manageable in size and attractive in shape. Good grooming also reduces the possibility of disease and helps flowering plants produce better blossoms. There are 2 methods for shaping plants: pinching and pruning.

Pinching
Use your thumb and forefinger to remove the young tip growth of a stem, and you are pinching the plant. This simple operation forces the plant to branch out below the pinch and become fuller and bushier.

Consider a young coleus plant, one started from seed or a cutting. If you do not pinch the plant during its active growth period, it will have one stem that grows straight up and eventually will become gangly, weak, and unattractive. To avoid this, nip out the growing tip as soon as the plant has 4 to 6 leaves. This will cause dormant buds to spring into active growth. Where you had one stem, now

you'll have two or more. After 2 or 3 weeks, pinch the tips of these new stems, and soon you'll have a bushy plant. Pinching is a handy skill to have in gardening. It works well for virtually all plants, but especially for soft-stemmed plants such as wax and angel-wing begonias, young geraniums, and coleus.

Pruning
Pruning is a slightly more complex operation that can shape a plant attractively and invigorate it. Pruning refers to removing young woody stems. When part of a plant is removed, the energy invested in sustaining that part is directed toward the rest of the plant. A sickly plant may be revived by pruning, and flowering plants encouraged to bloom.

If a stem is removed at its point of origin, the result will be opening up space within the stem framework. New growth will take place in the stems remaining or from the base of the plant. If the stem is cut off above a leaf, one or more new growth tips will grow near the pruned tip to make the plant denser.

Pinching encourages soft-stemmed plants to branch out and become fuller. Pinch out the tip of each new branch as it forms. Opposite: Use a small pruning shears to cut back woody growth and stimulate new branches on plants like camellias.

To prune properly, you will need a good pair of small hand pruners. With timely pruning, plants such as miniature rose, fuchsia, gardenia, and flowering maple will blossom more profusely and branch framework will be well balanced and sturdy. After a flowering period, clip off spent blooms and long, weak branches that extend beyond the plant's overall shape.

Cleaning

Plant foliage must be cleaned occasionally to rid the plant of insects, eggs, and mites. Cleaning also clears the stomata (openings on the underside of the leaf) of dust and other particles, facilitating the intake and release of gases, and allows the maximum amount of light to reach the plant.

Wash large-leaf plants with a damp cloth or sponge. Use a very mild solution of dishwashing soap and water to make the job easier. The soap will not harm plants, but oil can cause problems by clogging leaf pores.

Always be careful in cleaning your houseplants not to spread pests or disease from an infested plant to others. For example, if you are using a rag and clean a plant suffering from mites, disinfect the rag with a 1:10 solution of household bleach and water before cleaning other plants.

PLANT SUPPORTS

Stakes, trellises, and other means of support are necessary for certain houseplants. These ensure healthy, attractive growth for climbing or vining plants such as bougainvillea, monstera, and philodendrons.

Staking

Staking is used to train plants and to protect their fragile or elongated stems from breaking. Often, early in the life of a plant such as chrysanthemum, tuberous begonia, or poinsettia, each stem is tied to a stake (usually of dark green bamboo or wood). Important points to remember are to stake early (you can keep a straight stem straight, but you may not be able to uncrook a crooked one); use pieces of soft yarn, strips of cloth, or the commercial wire twist-ties to tie the stems;

Trellises

Although they are not seen frequently, trellises have a definite place in houseplant gardening. Vines grown on a trellis flourish while those that trail or hang grow more slowly because they lack the support they depend on. You can put up a small wood, wire, or string trellis wherever you want a vine to climb. In a sunny window, 'Heavenly Blue' morning glories or ivy geraniums make a cheerful drapery of flowers and foliage.

ARTIFICIAL LIGHTING

Abundant light is critical for healthy plant growth. Artificial light provides you with a constant and dependable source of light that will:

Encourage health and bloom;

Make it possible to grow plants in out-of-the-way or difficult places;

Help transform dark areas into attractive plant displays;

Pull your plants through long periods of cloudy weather that would otherwise inhibit growth.

With artificial light it's possible to have the same light intensity in December as in June, and since fluorescent light is cool, it will never burn plant foliage.

Types of Artificial Light

To choose the best artificial lighting for your plants, you need to know the differences between *incandescent* and *fluorescent* light.

Light can be broken down into different wavelengths that are perceived as colors. This is what happens when sunlight passes through a prism and breaks into bands of red, orange, yellow, green, blue, and violet—the range of colors called the *light spectrum*.

While it's believed that plants make use of all light waves, the most necessary to plant life are those at the ends of the spectrum, red and blue. Red rays stimulate flowering and affect other growth processes including stem length and leaf size. Blue and violet rays promote foliage growth. And both red and blue light waves play important roles in photosynthesis.

Because most homes today are lit by incandescent light, incandescent bulbs are cheaper and simpler to install than fluorescent lighting. However, they have some serious drawbacks in regard to plants: They project light that is not evenly distributed; they are relatively inefficient, requiring more energy to produce light; and they emit mostly red light waves and lack enough blue waves to meet plant needs. The chief disadvantage however, is that they generate heat that can dry the surrounding air and even scorch plants.

Fluorescent bulbs present several advantages over incandescent light.

Various fluorescent lamps emit different "colors." Top to bottom: Daylight, Deluxe warm white, warm white, and cool white.

Despite a higher initial cost and more complicated installation procedure, they are more economical in the long run because they produce more light on less energy. (A fluorescent tube produces 2½ to 3 times as much light as an incandescent bulb of the same wattage.) They produce less heat. They also produce light over a greater range of the spectrum, and mostly in the blue range.

Because incandescent bulbs are high in red light and low in blue, and common fluorescent tubes are exactly the opposite, many plant growers have used and advocated mixing incandescent and fluorescent lighting to cover the spectrum, especially in situations where the far-red light needed to trigger flowering is desired. Ordinary incandescent light is not recommended for this purpose, however;

if you want to supplement daylight or fluorescent light, use the reflectorized incandescent lights, or "cool beam" lights, which are designed to cut the heat projected onto plants by 50 percent. To illuminate a single specimen or a collection, cool beam incandescent floodlights can be placed as close as 12 inches from the leaves, depending on wattage. These must be used only in porcelain sockets in bullet (snap-in) or track (screw-in) installations. For plants with little or no natural light, leave these lights on 12 to 14 hours per day. As a supplement, a few hours every evening should suffice.

With the development of fluorescent tubes that emit more red light, it is possible to mix these with the tubes rich in the blue range. An ideal combination often recommended is one warm white (rich in the red spectrum) tube with one cool white tube.

There are many types of fluorescent tubes on the market, including a number developed specifically for growing plants. These vary greatly in the amount and quality of light they offer, factors that must be taken into consideration when you choose your lighting system.

Supplemental light spotlights these paper-white narcissus and allows them to bloom in a shady interior spot. Above: With artificial light propagating plants for indoors and outdoors is easy.

For sick plants and forcing flowering plants construct a simple plant care center. This one features timed lights which provide 12–14 hours of light a day. The reflecting shades increase the light level, humidity, and warmth. The open ends allow air to circulate freely.

Fluorescent Fixtures

The most common set up for growing plants under artificial light consists of a standard industrial fluorescent unit with a reflector. This unit can be adjusted to stand or hang 12 to 24 inches above the surface on which the plants will be placed. The light should be movable up and down in order to meet varied light intensity requirements. Plants on the same surface that have different requirements can be placed closer to the light by using supports such as wooden blocks.

For a sizable garden under lights, a prefabricated unit with several shelves makes a good investment. (The one drawback to this arrangement is that these lights are not adjustable, and the fixed intensity limits the types of plants that can be grown. The light may be too dim for some plants.) Using utilitarian steel shelving, you can construct a similar fluorescent light garden yourself at less expense.

A fluorescent fixture with two or three 40-watt tubes in a reflector will light a growing area 2 by 4 feet. Two such fixtures mounted parallel will illuminate a bench 3 by 4 feet. Two industrial fluorescent fixtures 8 feet long suspended side by side will light a bench 3 by 8 feet. Fixtures with 20-watt tubes provide less light but are still useful for growing plants; you simply need more tubes if you want equivalent light.

Fluorescent tubes should be lit 12 to 16 hours a day. Less time results in poor growth; more is harmful to plants. Most growers turn lights on at 7 or 8 a.m. and off at 10 or 11 p.m. Use an automatic timer for convenience and consistency.

To provide humidity for plants on a tabletop or bench under fluorescent lights, you can frame the surface and cover it with 1 to 2 inches of moist vermiculite, sand, pebbles, or perlite. If this is impractical, fill each pot saucer with pebbles and add water to just below the surface of the rocks. Shelves may be waterproofed by lining with heavy duty polyethylene or by using a galvanized tray made to fit. There are excellent plastic trays available that work well.

Care During Rest Periods

Nature's cycle for seasonal plant growth applies to indoor plants in somewhat the same way it applies to others: Shorter days and cooler temperatures often bring about a period of dormancy. Centrally heated indoor environments with artificial light offer the potential to create an endless summer for plants. However, some plants under regulated artificial light and temperatures have resting periods when growth slows and when, consequently, they need less food and water. It is most important that you realize when your pot plants are resting—or need a rest. This most likely will occur after a flush of new growth or a period of heavy flowering. Symptoms may include the absence of new growth, a drooping appearance, and yellowing, falling leaves.

When these symptoms appear, do not apply any fertilizer. Allow the plant to dry out a bit; don't keep it constantly damp. Tropical plants are especially apt to go dormant if situated where temperatures stay generally below 70°F. Cold temperatures, wet soil, and continuing to feed at the same level as in growth periods have all combined to kill countless pot plants. When seasons change and your plant needs a rest, do not repot it. If you think repotting is necessary, wait until the plant puts out some new leaf buds and shows signs of active growth.

Tuberous and bulbous plants often die back to the ground when they rest. In cultivation we simply withhold fertilizer and water. However, not all bulbous plants die down. Potted agapanthus, for example, stays leafy and green all year, sending up flowers after a period of active growth.

Tropical foliage plants are responsive to warm, moist air rather than to seasonal periods of long and short days. These plants will grow very slowly in winter unless your home is unusually warm and humid. Also, in these energy-conscious days when many thermostats are being lowered a few degrees, the growth of almost all houseplants will slow down in the colder months.

SUMMERTIME OUTDOORS

After a long, cold winter, your houseplants deserve a dose of fresh air, filtered sunlight, and rainwater. This treatment rejuvenates them and adds a fresh touch of greenery and color to your porch, patio, or yard with little trouble or expense for you.

To assure growth outdoors and minimize the attention you must give them, take only your hardiest plants out into the wilds of your backyard. Let the more delicate plants remain indoors; these will suffer from the wind and cold that can strike unexpectedly.

There are a few basic steps to the moving process that should be followed: Wait until all threat of frost has passed and temperatures do not go below 45°F at night. The transition must be gradual. Find a protected, well-shaded spot and keep them there for at least a week. Even with the shade, the increase in light intensity will be dramatic. After a couple of weeks, most plants can be moved to a location with filtered sunlight and protection from the wind.

During the first few weeks keep a close watch on your plants for evidence of excessive dryness, pest infestation, or shock.

You can display your plants outdoors in their containers or sink the pots below ground in your garden, provided the site has good drainage. Dig a bed 3 or 4 inches deeper than the pots and allow enough space to accommodate the foliage without overlapping. Layer the bed with 3 inches of gravel and an inch of peat moss. Set the pots into the bed and fill with soil up to the rims. The gravel should prevent the roots from spreading out the drainage holes, but in addition you may want to twist the pots in the ground periodically (every few weeks) to prevent rooting in the ground.

MOVING FROM OUTDOORS TO INDOORS

As summer wanes and temperatures begin to dip, prepare to bring your plants indoors. In addition, some garden flowers can be saved from frost and brought inside. There are many tender perennial flowers that we grow outdoors in warm weather as annuals. These can be brought in before frost for an extended flowering season. On a sunny window sill, under fluorescent lights, or in a home greenhouse, some continue to bloom indefinitely. For others this trip indoors is merely to capture a few more flowers before the plants die. For some plants, it is merely a holding operation meant to keep them alive (but not in active growth) until the following spring or summer, when once again they can be put outdoors.

If a plant is already growing in a pot or hanging basket of a size convenient to bring inside, the procedure is simple. Set it up on a bench or table where you can really see it, then clip off every yellowed leaf, spent flower, and seed pod. If the plant is too large for the space you have inside, study the branch structure and do some cutting back: Your aim is to retain a pleasing overall shape with as many healthy leaves and flower buds as possible and at the same time reduce its overall size.

Before bringing the plant inside, clean any dirt from it and from the outside of the pot. In addition, always examine the foliage carefully for pests and disease. You don't want to introduce them into your home, where they may infest your entire collection of plants. Treat any pests with the recommended pesticides according to the label directions. (For more information on pest control, see the chart on page 44 and 45.)

If both plant and container are too large to bring inside, potting down—moving the plant into a smaller pot—is in order. This procedure is illustrated in the photographs on this page.

Pot down large, straggly plants brought in from outside. Here we place a marigold in a smaller pot with fresh soil. Water thoroughly, then trim off the old growth and spent blooms to enjoy a healthier looking plant.

Primroses have few rivals when it comes to vibrant and colorful blooms. The strong light that enters through a southern exposure produces multitudes of blossoms.

Digging Plants from the Garden

Plants growing directly in the ground require careful transplanting if you wish to bring them indoors. These plants suffer more shock than those simply transferred in pots. The best time to dig up and pot a plant is 2 or 3 weeks before frost is expected. This allows for a period of recuperation and acclimation to the pot and to lower light. Place the newly potted plants in a shady, moist spot before the final move indoors. Depending on the size of the plant, use either a sturdy trowel or a spade. If the soil is dry, apply water a day or two before digging; this will make your work easier and also will spare some root damage. Dig up the plant with a good chunk of earth surrounding the root system, and follow the instructions for potting down.

Which Flowers to Save

Annual or tender perennial flowers that send up sturdy new basal growth whenever the tops are cut back are the best to save. These include wax or semperflorens begonia, petunia, and nicotiana. With careful transplanting and culture you can have success saving heal-thy flowering plants of geranium, heliotrope, ageratum, lobelia, French marigold, lantana, impatiens, torenia, browallia, sage, sweet alyssum, and verbena.

Annual phlox, zinnias, China asters, and tall African or hybrid marigolds are difficult indoors. All of these need some sunlight in fall and winter in order to continue flowering. Since they will have already been blooming for several months, it's too much to expect them to continue indefinitely.

In caring for these plants, keep the soil moist, feed every 2 weeks with a liquid houseplant fertilizer, and keep all spent blooms clipped off. You can extend blooming this way for weeks. Plants of this type are ideal for filling a new greenhouse while you are collecting and starting permanent seeds, cuttings, and bulbs.

While you are rescuing these flowers from frost, remember also to bring in frost-tender bulbs such as caladium, achimenes, tuberous begonia, and amaryllis. You can also pot up and keep in a sunny spot such herbs as borage, lemon verbena, sweet basil, marjoram, parsley, and scented geraniums.

DEALING WITH RELUCTANT BLOOMERS

It's often necessary to coax your flowering houseplants to bloom by giving them a little more tender loving care and attention than usual. The intensity and duration of light are critical to flower production. Because flowering is a special energy-consuming activity, most plants require more light during this time than that needed for maintenance. Often a plant that refuses to bloom isn't receiving enough light. A plant located near a northern exposure, where light is scarce, will usually have difficulty blooming.

Certain plants flower only after exposure to a particular daylength; this feature is called *photoperiodism*. When daylength is longer than a specific minimum, plants referred to as "long-day plants" respond by moving into their flower-producing mode. The daylight hours must be at least a specific number of hours or longer. Gloxinias and hibiscus are examples of long-day plants. Others referred to as "short-day plants" do just the reverse: They move into flower production when days are shorter than a certain maximum; that is, a specific number of daylight hours or less. Chrysanthemums are short-day plants requiring a period of 10 hours or less of light per day (at least 14 hours of total darkness) before they can flower. Interrupting the long dark period with just a few minutes of light will prevent flowering in short-day plants and may permit flowering in long-day plants.

You may ask, "How do florists get poinsettias to bloom just in time for Christmas, and why can't I do the same?" Poinsettias, Christmas cactus, and chrysanthemums are "triggered" to bloom by the commercial grower so they can be available at holiday times and during winter. Growers induce poinsettias, which are short-day plants, to bloom by covering them with black cloth during some of the daylight hours in early fall. The simulation of winter sends the plant into its cycle of producing flowers.

Because the artificial lighting of most homes suspends the seasonal light changes and eliminates the long periods of total darkness that winter provides, you'll have to start altering the amount of light that reaches your poinsettia beginning in early October. Place the plant in a room with only natural light, cover it with a light-tight box, or place it in a light-tight closet. If you give it total darkness for 12 hours per day, it will bloom for Christmas—but be careful not to skip any days or your efforts will fail.

With most flowering pot plants from the florist, one season of bloom is all you can expect. It's doubtful that you'll be able to do much more with them than sustain their current flowers. After a few weeks or perhaps months, the flowers will fade and the leaves will droop. The plants will not flower again because the special greenhouse conditions required are so difficult to duplicate in the home.

Houseplants in flower generally need more water, especially if you have placed them in a high light or heat or low humidity situation, which spurs the plant to transpire more rapidly. Make sure that your plants do not suffer from poor drainage. Most flowering houseplants prefer slightly dry roots before they'll produce buds. Once a plant has been induced to flower, it should be watered thoroughly and regularly. Pay special attention to its watering needs at this time.

During the flowering period plants need fertilizer with a lower proportion of nitrogen, the nutrient that aids foliage growth. The lack of nitrogen triggers bud formation. The ratio of elements in your fertilizer should change from high nitrogen and low phosphorus and potassium to low nitrogen and high levels of phosphorus and potas-sium. Fertilizers specifically formulated for flowering plants have these proportions.

Pruning and shaping enhance flower production, but don't get carried away with the job and prune so much or so often that no buds can form. Plants also need to be pinched back after blossoming.

If you have provided all these environmental conditions and your plants still don't flower, consider the following questions:

Is the plant in a container too large for its roots?

A potbound houseplant is more likely to flower because it has little room to develop roots and the energy that has gone into root production is now invested in growth above ground.

Has the plant been transplanted recently?

Transplanting disrupts the plant's normal growing routine and also will give the roots more room to grow. Instead of transplanting just before flowering occurs, replace the top third of the soil with new mix.

Is the plant immature?

New plants may simply be too young to produce flowers.

Is the soil pH below 5.0 or above 8.0?

If the pH is 5.0 or below, certain toxic ions become available to the plant and impair its growth. A pH reading above 8.0 makes some micronutrients, such as iron and manganese, unavailable for healthy plant growth.

Is your plant in its dormant period?

Be patient. Don't try to rush this slow process along; a plant needs to rest before it can flower.

When all else fails, try putting the plant under stress by cutting back on water. The plant will respond to this threat by producing offspring that will survive it. Let the plant become dry, but don't continue the treatment if it wilts severely and no buds appear. In all cases, once buds show, resume normal care and don't disorient the plant by moving it.

Poinsettias make a cheerful, traditional winter table arrangement.

PESTS AND PROBLEMS

Inspect your plants each time you water to spot any problems, pests, and diseases before they do extensive damage. Use this chart to solve any problems that occur.

Insects are usually brought indoors on new plants. Check new plants carefully before placing them in your home. If you need to use a pesticide, take care to follow the directions precisely and always check the label of the pesticide to be sure that it is suitable for the plant and the pest you are treating. Apply houseplant sprays formulated for indoor use. If you use a recommended pesticide that is not strictly for indoor use be sure to take your infested plant outdoors and spray in a shady area.

CULTURAL PROBLEMS

Lack of Light

Problem: New growth is weak and spindly with large gaps between the leaves. If most of the available light is coming from one direction plants bend their stems and leaves in that direction.

Solution: Gradually move the plant to a brighter location. Most plants will tolerate direct sun if they are kept well watered. However, if they are allowed to dry while in direct sunlight, they will sunburn. If a brighter location is not available, provide artificial light as described on pages 38 to 40.

Nitrogen Deficiency

Problem: The oldest leaves—usually the lower leaves—turn yellow and may drop. Yellowing starts at the leaf margins and progresses inward without producing a distinct pattern. The yellowing may progress upward until only the newest leaves remain green. Growth is slow, new leaves are small, and the whole plant may be stunted.

Solution: For a quick response, spray the leaves with a foliar fertilizer such as Ra-Pid-Gro plant food. Fertilize houseplants with a 5–10–5 fertilizer. Add the fertilizer at regular intervals, as recommended on the label.

Salt Damage

Problem: The leaf margins of plants with broad leaves or the leaf tips of plants with long, narrow leaves turn brown and die. This browning occurs on the older leaves first, but when the condition is severe, new leaves may also be affected. On some plants, the older leaves may turn yellow and die.

Solution: Leach excess salts from the soil by flushing with water. See page 36.

Sunburn or Bleaching

Problem: Dead tan or brown patches develop on leaves that are exposed to direct sunlight. Or, leaf tissue may lighten or turn gray. In some cases, the plant remains green, but growth is stunted. Damage is most severe when the plant is allowed to dry out.

Solution: Move plants that cannot tolerate direct sun to a shaded spot. Or cut down the light intensity by closing the curtains when direct sun shines on the plant. Prune off badly damaged leaves or trim away damaged leaf areas to improve the plant's appearance. Keep plants properly watered.

Too Little Water

Problem: Leaves are small, and plant fails to grow well. Growth may be stunted. Plant parts or the whole plant may wilt. Margins of leaves or tips of leaves of narrow-leafed plants may dry and become brittle, but still retain a dull green color. Bleached areas may occur between the veins. Such tissues may die and remain bleached, or turn tan or brown. Plant may die.

Solution: Water plants immediately and thoroughly. If the soil is completely dry, add a bit of wetting agent (available at garden centers) or soak the entire pot in water for a couple of hours.

Too Much Water or Poor Drainage

Problem: Plants fail to grow and may be wilting. Leaves lose their glossiness and may become light green or yellow. An examination of the rootball reveals brown, mushy roots without white tips. The soil in the bottom of the pot may be very wet and may have a foul odor. Plants may die.

Solution: Discard severely wilted plants and those without white root tips. Do not water less severely affected plants until the soil is barely moist. Prevent the problem by using light soil mixes with good drainage.

Water Spots

Problem: Small, light tan to reddish brown, somewhat angular spots appear on the upper surfaces of the leaves. These spots are scattered and are found most frequently on the older leaves.

Solution: Avoid getting cold water on the leaves when watering. Tepid water will not spot the leaves.

Aphids

Problem: Leaves are curling, discolored, and reduced in size. A shiny or sticky substance may coat the leaves. Tiny, nonwinged, green soft-bodied insects cluster on the buds, young stems, and leaves.

Solution: Use an indoor plant insect spray containing Orthene, resmethrin, or pyrethrins.

Botrytis Grey Mold

Problem: Brown spots and blotches appear on the leaves and possibly on the stems. Spots on flowers may be white, tan, brown, or purple, or the natural color of the flower may be intensified. If stems are infected, they may rot, causing the top part of the plant to topple and die. Under humid conditions, the infected portions may be covered with a fuzzy gray or brown growth.

Solution: Remove all diseased and dead plant material promptly, particularly old flowers. Avoid splashing water on the foliage and flowers, and avoid growing plants under crowded conditions where air is damp and still. Provide good air circulation around plants, but protect them from cold drafts. If the problem persists, grow plants in a warmer spot.

Fungus Gnats

Problem: Small, slender, dark insects fly around when plants are disturbed. They frequently run across the foliage and soil, and may also be found on windows. Roots may be damaged, and seedlings may die.

Solution: Spray with a houseplant insect spray containing diazinon. Repeated applications may be necessary.

Greenhouse Whitefly

Problem: Tiny, winged insects feed mainly on the undersides of the leaves. The insects are covered with white waxy powder. When the plant is touched, insects flutter around it. Leaves may be mottled and yellow.

Solution: Spray with houseplant insect sprays containing Orthene, resmethrin, malathion, or diazinon. Check labels to determine which material can be used on your particular plant. Spray weekly as long as the problem persists. Remove heavily infested leaves as soon as the problem is spotted. If only a few leaves are infested, wipe off larvae with a damp cloth or cotton swabs soaked in alcohol.

Mealybugs

Problem: White cottony or waxy insects are on the undersides of the leaves, on the stems, and particularly in the crotches or where leaves are attached. The insects tend to congregate, resulting in a cottony appearance. Cottony masses that contain eggs of the insects may also be present. A sticky substance may cover the leaves or drop onto surfaces below the plant. Infested plants are unsightly, do not grow well, and may die if severely infested.

Solution: Control of mealybugs is difficult. The waxy coverings on the insects and egg sacs and the tendency for the insects to group together protect them from insecticides. Thoroughly spray stems and both sides of leaves with a houseplant insect spray containing Orthene or resmethrin and oil or spray outdoors with a mix containing Orthene, malathion, or diazinon.
  If only a few mealybugs are present, wipe them off with a damp cloth, or use cotton swabs dipped in rubbing alcohol. Carefully check all parts of the plant to make sure all insects are removed. Wipe off any egg sacs under the rims or bottoms of pots. Discard severely infested plants, and avoid taking cuttings from such plants. Inspect new plants before putting them in the house.

Scale Insects

Problem: Nodes, stems, and leaves are covered with white, cottony, cushionlike masses or brown, crusty bumps or clusters of somewhat flattened reddish gray or brown scaly bumps. The bumps can be scraped or picked off easily. Leaves turn yellow and may drop. A shiny or sticky material may cover the leaves.

Solution: Spraying is most effective against the crawlers rather than against adults. Spray with a houseplant insect spray containing Orthene or resmethrin and oil or spray outdoors with a mix containing diazinon, malathion, or Orthene as soon as the insects are spotted. Repeated applications may be necessary.

Spider Mites

Problem: Leaves are stippled, yellowing, and dirty. Leaves may dry out and drop. There may be webbing over the flower buds, between leaves, or on the lower surfaces of the leaves. To determine whether a plant is infested with mites, hold a sheet of white paper underneath an affected leaf and tap the leaf sharply. Minute green, red, or yellow specks the size of pepper grains will drop to the paper and begin to crawl around. The pests are easily seen against the white background.

Solution: Spray infested plants with an indoor plant insect spray containing Orthene, resmethrin and oil, or pyrethrins. Plants need to be sprayed weekly for several weeks to kill the mites as they hatch from the eggs. To avoid introducing mites into your house, inspect newly purchased plants carefully.

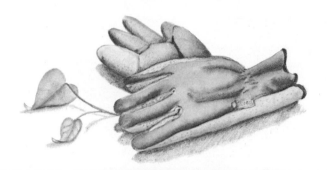

PROPAGATION

Techniques for growing new plants ❧ Rooting stem and leaf cuttings ❧ Dividing plants ❧ Forcing bulbs ❧ Annuals and perennials to grow indoors

Propagation—the creation of new plants from old—is one of the most rewarding, easy, and economical ways to support your plant-growing habit. Besides saving you money, propagating your own plants gives you direct control over the quality of your plants as well as providing you the enjoyable experience of being involved with them from their first days of growth.

Plants propagate in two fundamentally different ways—sexually and asexually. Sexual propagation occurs when the male and female parts of the plant unite to produce seeds. Asexual propagation, also known as vegetative propagation, occurs when a piece of a plant is cultivated and grown. The new plant is simply a young extension of the original parent plant.

There are a wide array of vegetative propagation techniques. The one you choose depends on the specific plant you wish to propagate and the method you prefer. The following discussion will help familiarize you with the various techniques and the types of plants suitable to each.

DIVISION

This technique involves dividing one entire plant, including its root system and foliage, into two or more separate plants. Plants that have multiple basal stems, or stems

Propagating leaves from piggyback and heartleaf philodendron makes an attractive display near a bright window.

emerging from the same central point at the base of the plant, are said to grow in the rosette form. This includes plants such as the cast iron plant, spider plant, most ferns, wax begonias, most bromeliads, cluster-forming succulents like certain sedums and crassulas, and African violets. When multiple stems emerge from the base of a plant, you can divide it. Foliage plants should be divided in the early spring when the plants are just beginning to produce new growth. If your environmental conditions are moderately warm and humid you can divide a plant anytime. Flowering plants are best divided during their dormant periods when they are not flowering.

The easiest way to propagate by division is to take a sharp knife and slice down through the rootball, severing a new plant from the old. Remember that you must get some of the main root and stem systems in each new division, or the plants cannot live. Plant divisions immediately and water thoroughly to prevent the roots from drying out. Keep them in bright light out of direct sun. Water the plants frequently until they root and appear upright and healthy. Then place them in their permanent location and resume normal care.

Often these rosette plants will produce offsets, which are small plants that are still attached to the parent. They can be separated and planted in the same manner as a division.

Another way to divide is to knock the entire plant out of its pot, rinse off the soil surrounding the roots, then gently break apart the divisions by hand and replant each one.

Tuber Division

This is closely related to dividing plants with multiple basal stems or leaf rosettes. Tuber division works for large bulbs of gloxinia, tuberous begonia, and caladium. Simply cut the tuber as you would a seed potato, being sure that every part has a bud, or "eye." Dust the cut surface with fungicide and plant each piece in a moist rooting medium.

OFFSETS ON STOLONS

Several common houseplants reproduce by sending out miniature new plants on runners or shoots. Some examples are spider plant, rosary vine, flame violet, and some species of African violet. Offsets of these are ready to be divided from the parent when they begin to form aerial roots at their bases.

One method for rooting an offset on a stolon is to fill a small pot with moist rooting medium and place it alongside the parent plant. Lay the plantlet on the soil in the new pot without severing the stolon (or runner); hairpin or wire the stolon into place. Active new growth will signal that the young plant has rooted and you can sever it from the parent. An alternative method of dividing the plantlet from the parent is to clip the stolon off and insert

Propagate spider plants by rooting new plants, offsets, that grow on the stolens.

the base of the plantlet into a moist propagating medium. Cover with glass or plastic film until new roots have formed.

Unlike most other plants that propagate by stolons, the piggyback plant forms new plantlets on top of mature leaves, but these are rooted in the same manner as stolons.

STEM CUTTINGS

Inducing a cutting to form roots is the most popular method of vegetative propagation. Cut a piece of branch, remove the lower leaves, plant the stem in a rooting medium, and wait until roots form. Once several branched roots have formed, it is ready to be planted in a pot. This basic method varies, depending on the plant you root and the conditions in which you choose to propagate it. Most plants with soft stems, such as impatiens, are easy to propagate by this method. Others with woody stems, such as the older growth on camellias, are more difficult.

First let's discuss a few requirements that are essential for your cuttings to root successfully. Different gardeners use different rooting mediums for cuttings. In all cases it is important that the medium holds a lot of water and is coarse, so that air can circulate through the material and reach the roots. One of the best rooting mediums is a mixture of 1 part sand and 1 part peat moss. You also can use straight vermiculite, perlite, milled sphagnum moss, or 10 parts perlite to 1 part peat moss.

One method for rooting cuttings is to simply place them in a glass of water. Water-rooted cuttings can be transplanted into one of the soilless mixes such as the University of California or Cornell formula (see page 18). Do not use potting soil as a rooting medium; it is too rich for the immature roots your cuttings will sprout.

Plastic pots are preferable to clay pots for cuttings because they retain moisture for a longer period of time.

If you want to root a number of different cuttings, a clear plastic bread box or shoe storage box makes an excellent propagator. Use a heated ice pick to punch a few ventilation holes in the top. Add 2 inches of rooting medium to the bottom, moisten, then insert your cuttings. Replace the lid and set the box in a bright, warm place out of direct sun. You can make a similar propagating box using a seed flat or fruit lug to hold the cuttings. A sheet of polyethylene plastic held up by wire coat hangers makes the "greenhouse" cover. A sheet of glass also works well as a cover.

If you read your seed catalogs closely or wander down garden center aisles reading labels, you may have noticed small containers of rooting hormone. These are excellent products and do promote faster rooting and better root systems, especially in woody plants. You don't really need a rooting hormone for plants such as coleus or Swedish ivy, which root quickly and easily; but plants with slightly woody stems—for example, fuchsia

and miniature rose—are much more apt to root if a hormone is used.

The procedure for taking and rooting a cutting is as follows:

Wet the rooting medium and let it drain. Use a sharp knife or razor blade to cut off a healthy piece of growth, usually 4 to 6 inches long. Cut at an angle just below a *node*, the joint from which both leaves and new roots normally arise. Remove the lower 2 or 3 leaves and any buds you find on your cutting. If the cutting has many leaves, remove enough that none will come into contact with the rooting medium; this can sometimes cause leaves to decay. Dust the cutting end with some hormone powder. Use your index finger or a pencil to make a hole in the rooting medium and insert the bare stem portion of the cutting. Firm it in place. It is important to plant the cutting quickly after severing it from the mother plant. Often cuttings fail to root because they dry out before being planted. Encase the entire cutting and container in a plastic bag. Use a stake or a loop of wire to support the plastic so it does not touch the foliage. Finally, set the cutting in a bright, warm place. Do not place it in direct sunlight.

You can tell when roots have begun to grow because the foliage will perk up and the new plant will put out new growth. Also, if you tug gently on the cutting it will not pull out of the soil. Remove the plastic cover, at first for an hour or two daily, then for several hours, and finally discard the cover and move the plant to its permanent growing conditions.

The time needed for the rooting process varies from 1 to 6 weeks depending on the plant. The best way to determine when the plant is ready to be transplanted is to check the roots. Gently lift the cutting out of the rooting medium and observe the root length. The roots should not be much longer than an inch or they likely will tear off when you transplant the cutting. It is important to move these new plants out of the sterile rooting medium and into soil as soon as possible. There is some danger of nutrient deficiency and root rot if cuttings are left too long in rooting medium.

LEAF CUTTINGS

Some plants have the amazing ability to propagate themselves from a single leaf cutting. Best known for this is the African violet, but the same technique works for rex begonias, gloxinias, sedums, kalanchoes, and even some philodendrons and peperomias.

To take a leaf cutting from a milky-stem plant such as a poinsettia or geranium, make the cut, then rub the cut end with alcohol (to prevent disease) and allow it to dry or callous for a few hours. Place the cutting on the kitchen cabinet or somewhere else out of direct sun. When the cut end is dry, proceed with planting.

ROOTING TREE AND SHRUB CUTTINGS

Trees and shrubs can be propagated from *softwood* or *hardwood* cuttings. Softwood describes this year's growth taken early or midseason. Hardwood describes growth at the end of the season.

Softwood cuttings to try include flowering maple, Norfolk Island pine, gardenia, and rose. These are prepared for planting in the same manner as stem cuttings. They do best in a cool, moist, bright, and well-ventilated atmosphere, with no direct sun until the roots have formed. Some growers rig up a mist system with jets timed to mist the cuttings every few minutes.

Hardwood cuttings are usually made in autumn, sometimes after frost has defoliated the deciduous types. Dip the base of each cutting in rooting hormone, then plant. Cover with plastic or glass and keep moderately cool (60° to 70°F). A cool fluorescent-light garden, perhaps in a basement, makes an ideal spot to root hardwood cuttings.

GROWING PLANTS FROM SEED

A few houseplants such as asparagus ferns and primroses are easily raised from seed, but most require time, skill, and heated conditions for success—something most of us, unless we are professional horticulturists, do not have.

A seed is a tiny dormant plant waiting for the right conditions to begin its life cycle. To achieve this it must be given a disease-free growing medium, proper warmth and moisture, and adequate light for germination.

Seeds for houseplants are available from most quality seed sources. They may be sown by the same methods used for outdoor plants, with bottom heat (70° to 75°F) added to expedite germination. Bottom heat is a method of heating the planting area from below with electric coils. Inexpensive soil heating cables are available in various sizes to meet your needs. A garden center can often secure the best type of unit for your use.

An easy way to start seeds is to sow them in moistened vermiculite or in milled sphagnum moss. Both are available at garden supply centers. Use flats, cartons, pots, or any container you desire. Tiny dustlike seeds are scattered on top of the moist growing medium. Sow seeds sparingly so that seedlings don't get crowded and reduce the air circulation. Cover them to a depth twice their own diameter. Firm the vermiculite or sphagnum around the seed by pressing gently. Label each type of seed with name, date planted, and any other desired information. Water lightly and slip the seed tray into a plastic bag or cover it with paper. Small plastic "greenhouses"—trays with clear plastic covers—make excellent seed propagators. Read seed packets to see if light is required for germination. Follow the directions and check seeds daily, adding water if necessary.

When seedlings emerge move them to brighter light. The first 2 leaves to sprout are not true leaves but rather *cotyledons*, which nourish

Salvage leggy plants that do not have lower leaves through the process of *air layering*. Cut halfway into the stem. Insert a wedge to prop the stem open. Wrap with plastic filled with moist sphagnum and secure around the stem. Within a few months roots will appear and the rooted stem portion can be cut off and potted. Below: Bottom heating by electric coils.

EASY PLANTS TO PROPAGATE FROM SEED

Botanical name	Common name
Aglaonema modestum	Chinese evergreen
Allium schoenoprasum	Chives
Begonia semperflorens	Begonia
Bromeliads	
Cacti	
Chlorophytum comosum	Spider plant
Cyclamen persicum	Cyclamen
Dracaena fragrans 'Massangeana'	Dracaena
Sinningia speciosa	Gloxinia
Peperomia species	Peperomia
Saintpaulia species	African violet

Given a few seed packets, some containers, potting mix, and a little guidance, children can experience the thrill of growing their own plants from seeds. Choose some easy plants from the adjacent chart.

the stem tip and the foliage leaves (true leaves) that follow. Wait for foliage leaves to appear before placing the seedlings in sunshine, then give them the same light you would the mature plant. Foliage plant seedlings thrive under a pair of 40-watt fluorescent tubes burned 16 hours each day. Special units are available in several sizes or you can buy the tubes and fixtures and build your own. Adjust the height of the lamps as necessary during growth.

When seedlings are 3 to 4 weeks old, fertilize them every two weeks with a diluted liquid solution (⅓ to ½ regular strength).

Transplant the seedlings when they have at least 4 true leaves. Dig them out carefully and place them into individual 2¼-inch pots filled with synthetic soil.

GROWING FERNS FROM SPORES

Unlike most plants, ferns produce dustlike spores, not seeds. It's a challenge to try to germinate these spores at home. Brush them into a paper bag from ripe spore–cases, which are found on the undersides of the fronds. Allow them to dry for a couple of weeks.

One spore germinating trick found especially successful is the brick and bread box method. Place a brick in a transparent bread box. Add 2 inches of water and add water as needed to maintain this level while spores are germinating. Cover the top of the brick with ¼-inch milled peat moss. Sprinkle the spores on top of this layer of moss and then cover the box with a glass

or plastic top to retain moisture.

Place the box in a dimly lit spot with moderate temperatures (65° to 75°F) for several months. A mosslike growth will appear on the top of the covered brick. This is the sexual stage of ferns. At this stage, transplant in 1-inch squares to a flat filled with all-purpose potting soil. Soon small ferns will appear in the flat. These can be planted in individual pots when they reach 2 to 3 inches in height.

FORCING BULBS

One rewarding aspect of indoor gardening is that you can persuade plants to bloom out of season. By duplicating—but shortening—the stages bulbs go through in your garden, you can have tulips, daffodils, and hyacinths blooming in the house while the wind drifts snow outdoors. People in warmer climates can also enjoy these spring bulbs ahead of time.

There are also some hardy perennials that respond to this forcing treatment—hosta, astilbe, bleeding heart, and lily of the valley.

Annual flowers can also be forced and kept in a sunny indoor garden, as can branches of favorite flowering shrubs.

How to Force Hardy Bulbs

It's easy to force tulips, daffodils, hyacinths, and the little bulbs—crocuses and grape hyacinths—to bloom indoors ahead of their normal time outdoors. Grow them as Christmas gifts for friends. Buy the largest bulbs you can find of the

type you wish to grow. Read the catalogs carefully to select those varieties recommended for forcing, or buy the ones we list. Most retail nurseries and garden centers will carry bulbs for forcing in the fall. For those bulbs you can't find in your local store use mail order catalogs. Order by September so the bulbs will be delivered in early fall. Then follow these steps:

Prepare a growing medium of equal parts soil, builder's sand, and peat moss. To each 5-inch pot of this mix, add a teaspoon of bone meal. If you don't want the bother of mixing soil, buy or mix an all-purpose medium. (For instructions on how to mix your own soil, see page 18.)

Pot size depends on the type and quantity of bulbs. One large daffodil or tulip bulb can be planted in a 4- or 5-inch pot in which three crocuses or other smaller bulbs would otherwise fit. For six tulips, daffodils, or hyacinths, you'll need an 8- to 10-inch pot. When you plant these large bulbs, cover the tops of tulips and hyacinths with an inch of soil; however, do not cover the necks and tops of daffodils. Cover the smaller bulbs, like crocuses, with an inch of soil, then water thoroughly.

Bulbs need a period of coolness after potting so that they can form a vigorous root system. Without a potful of roots, they cannot bloom prolifically later on. (It is also possible to purchase preplanted containers of bulbs conditioned to begin the forcing process.) Tradition

BULB VARIETIES FOR FORCING

Type	Color	Flowering Time
Crocus		
Remembrance	Purple	Winter and Spring
Purpureus grandiflorus	Purple	Winter and Spring
Flower Record	Purple	Late Winter, Spring
Victor Hugo	Purple	Winter and Spring
Peter Pan	White	Winter and Spring
Joan of Arc	White	Winter and Spring
Pickwick	Striped	Winter and Spring
Large Yellow	Yellow	Spring
Hyacinthus		
Jan Bos	Red	Winter
Pink Pearl	Pink	Winter and Spring
Lady Derby	Pink	Winter
Anne Marie	Pink	Winter
Amsterdam	Pink	Winter and Spring
Marconi	Pink	Spring
L'Innocence	White	Winter
Colosseum	White	Winter
Carnegie	White	Spring
Delft Blue	Blue	Winter
Ostara	Blue	Winter and Spring
Blue Jacket	Blue	Spring
Marie	Blue	Spring
Bismarck	Blue	Winter
Amethyst	Violet	Spring
Iris reticulata		
Harmony	Blue	Winter and Spring
Danfordiae	Yellow	Winter
Hercules	Purple	Winter and Spring
Muscari (Grape hyacinth)		
Early Giant	Blue	Winter and Spring
Narcissus		
Carlton	Yellow	Winter
Unsurpassable	Yellow	Winter and Spring
Joseph MacLeod	Yellow	Winter
Dutch Master	Yellow	Winter and Spring
Soleil d'Or	Yellow	Winter and Spring
Mt. Hood	White	Winter and Spring
Paper-white	White	Winter and Spring
Chinese Sacred lily	White	Winter and Spring
Barrett Browning	Orange cup/white perianth	Winter and Spring
Fortune	Bicolor	Winter
Ice Follies	Cream cup, white perianth	Winter and Spring
Magnet	Yellow trumpet, white perianth	Spring
Tulipa		
Bing Crosby	Red	Winter and Spring
Olaf	Red	Winter and Spring
Paul Richter	Red	Winter
Prominence	Red	Late Winter
Charles	Red	Winter
Stockholm	Red	Winter
Bellona	Yellow	Winter
Ornament	Yellow	Spring
Thule	Yellow with red	Winter
Hibernia	White	Winter and Spring
Christmas Marvel	Pink	Winter
Peerless Pink	Pink	Spring
Preludium	Pink	Winter
Kees Nelis	Red variagated with yellow or cream	Winter
Golden Eddy	Red, var. with yellow or cream	Spring
Karel Doorman	Red var. with yellow or cream	Winter

has it that you bury these pots of bulbs in a bed of cinders outdoors in a coldframe, leaving them there until at least New Year's Day (except some bulbs conditioned to bloom for Christmas). This system is impractical for most of us today, and besides, there are easier ways to accomplish the same thing.

Find a cool, frost-free place where bulbs can be forced. A garage that is attached to the house, but not heated, is a good place for bulbs to form roots. A cool attic or basement also will do. A temperature range of 35° to 55°F will promote root growth. Keep the soil evenly moist throughout this period.

You can start forcing the bulbs when sprouts begin to push up through the soil, usually sometime after January 1. Bring the pots indoors, a few each week so you will have blooms over a longer period of time, and place them in a sunny, cool (55° to 70°F) spot. Never allow the soil to dry out. The cooler the air, the longer the flowers will last. Keep bulbs away from sources of heat, such as radiators and gas heaters. Bring all pots into a warm and sunny location by late February.

Problems in forcing bulbs are few, but here are some that might occur:

■ Tulips almost always show some aphids, either on the leaves when they emerge from the soil, or on the flower buds. See "Pests and Problems" chart on page 44 and 45.

■ Flower buds of forced bulbs will blast (fail to open) if the soil is allowed to dry out severely after they've begun to grow.

■ Sometimes bulbs have basal rot; this is seldom your fault. If foliage suddenly turns yellow and stops growing, give it a gentle tug. Chances are you'll find it loose in the pot, and a rootless rotted bulb in the soil. Burn the bulb to destroy it and prevent the disease from spreading to other plants. After the flowers fade, keep the foliage in good health by providing moisture and sunlight. As soon as any danger of hard freezing is past, move them to an out-of-the-way place outdoors where the foliage can continue to mature and store up strength for another year's blooms. Although the bulbs will not stand forcing a second year, you will find them useful additions for the outdoor garden. Plant them there when you bring them from the house, or leave them in pots until the following autumn, transferring them then to the open ground. Store the bulbs in a cool, dark, ventilated place if you need the pots before autumn.

Narcissus

No matter where you live, *Narcissus* (daffodils) are delightful subjects for forcing indoors in a semisunny to sunny location. The bulbs are available in autumn. Plant them in moist pebbles in a bowl, or pot them in a mixture of equal parts soil, sand, and peat moss, kept moist. Either way, place the bases of the bulbs to a depth of 1 to 1½ inches in the growing medium, then water thoroughly. Drain and set away in a cool (50° to 65°F), dark place until the roots form. After the bulbs have a good root system—which usually takes 2 to 4 weeks—they may be brought into warmth and bright sun. Here they will quickly send up fragrant clusters of white or gold blossoms.

Discard paper-white narcissus after forcing if you live where winter cold dips below 20°F. In the South, plant them in the garden outdoors. But don't try to force them again. Buy new stock each year for forcing.

Hyacinths

The hyacinth bulb will grow in water if placed in specially designed containers or jars, or in any vase that will hold the bulb in the top and allow the roots to reach into the bottom section. Fill the vase so the base of the bulb is just above the water. Add water as needed to maintain this level. Change the water every 3 or 4 weeks. A small piece of charcoal in the water will keep it sweet and prevent harmful bacteria from developing. Place in a dark, cool area before moving to light. Use any of the varieties listed on page 51.

FORCING FLOWERING BRANCHES

The delicate beauty of long, willowy apple, cherry, forsythia, pussy willow, and flowering quince branches can bring springtime beauty indoors in the midst of winter. Two- to three-foot branches should be cut during the first two or three months of the year.

Be careful when cutting not to ruin the shape of the tree or shrub. Also, do not cut branches until the tiny buds begin to swell in late winter. If cut too soon the flowers will not open. Smash the cut ends of the branches with a hammer to help the branches absorb more water (except in the case of pussy willows, which should not be placed in water). Place all others in a large container of water in a moderately cool (60° to 70°F), bright room. Change the water every few days. In about two weeks the fragile blossoms will appear.

FORCING ANNUAL FLOWERS

Some of summer's brightest annual flowers force easily indoors in a lo-

Blooming purple hyacinths complement houseplants with their early spring color.

cation with full sun and a moderately cool, moist atmosphere. (Browallia and torenia will do with less sun—good east sunlight is ample.) In addition to making your own indoor garden colorful, they will make cheerful gifts for friends.

A temperature range of 60° to 70°F is ideal for forced annuals. Pot them in a mixture of equal parts soil, sand, and peat moss, and keep evenly moist.

Fertilize every 2 weeks with liquid houseplant food. Pinch growing tips as necessary to encourage compact plants. Aphids are likely to be troublesome. For control tips see page 44 and 45.

To grow ageratum, sweet alyssum, dwarf balsam, browallia, and dwarf cockscomb indoors for winter and early spring bloom, sow seeds in early August. The same is true for dwarf marigolds, sweet peas, nasturtiums, and morning glories. Transplant to individual pots as soon as seedlings are large enough. As they fill one pot with roots, transfer them to a larger size, stopping with 5- to 7-inch containers. Provide a trellis or strings for morning glory and sweet pea vines. Try hanging baskets for the trailing plants.

To grow lobelia, flowering tobacco, petunia, snapdragon, torenia, and verbena indoors, dig plants from the outdoor garden before frost in autumn. Disturb roots as little as possible and plant in 5- to 10-inch containers. Cut back leaves and stems severely to encourage strong new growth. Keep plants in shade and coolness for a few days while they accustom themselves to the pots. Then place in a sunny window and keep moist.

FORCING HARDY PERENNIALS

This is a specialized area of gardening that few ever try. However, if you have a perennial border that abounds with hosta, bleeding heart, astilbe, or lily-of-the-valley, try your hand at forcing these one winter. Here's how you do it:

Dig vigorous clumps in early fall, trim them back, and pot in a moist mixture of soil, sand, and peat moss. Then put them in a coldframe, unheated garage, or cool attic, where severe freezing will not occur. In mid-January or early February, begin to bring the pots indoors to a moderately cool (60° to 65°F), sunny window sill. Keep the soil evenly moist. When leaf growth becomes active, fertilize every 2 weeks with regular houseplant food. If all goes well, you will be rewarded with some of spring's loveliest flowers weeks, even months, out of season.

After forcing hardy perennials, replant them in the garden outdoors. Do not try to force the same clumps again for at least 2 years.

Daffodils are delightful subjects for forcing indoors in a sunny location. Above: Cinerarias blossom indoors if they receive plenty of sunlight.

THE GALLERY OF HOUSEPLANTS

Descriptions of all your favorite indoor plants ❧ Specific growing temperatures ❧ Water needs ❧ Light requirements ❧ Ideal soil mixes ❧ Problems to avoid

Today nurseries, flower shops, plant stores, supermarkets, even dime stores carry hundreds of different houseplants all the time. Confronting the rows and rows of plants to make a selection can be downright bewildering if not discouraging, especially if you are unfamiliar with plants or undecided about what you want and can grow. To help you sort through the multitude of plants available, we have organized a gallery of distinctive and popular houseplants.

Just as paintings in an art gallery may be hung with other paintings of a similar nature or period, we have organized the plants into 8 sections:

Bromeliads
Cacti
Ferns
Flowering Houseplants
Foliage Houseplants
Palms
Philodendrons
Succulents

The most general sections "Flowering Houseplants" and "Foliage Houseplants" include a wide range of species and varieties commonly available for growing indoors. The other 6 sections fall within these first 2 categories, but we are highlighting these popular plant groups by setting them off in their own sections for easy reference. This will enable you to compare their appearances and care requirements more easily than if the different types were spread throughout the collection. Each of these sections features a general discussion of the group and its care requirements, followed by brief descriptions of the many species and varieties readily available.

With an idea of what type of plant you want to learn more about, whether your idea be as general as a flowering houseplant or as specific as a fern, you can turn to the appropriate section and see photographs and read descriptions of the plants included in the group. Compare the appearance, the care requirements, and the environmental needs of the plants that appeal to you, and then make an informed preliminary selection before you go to the store to purchase a plant.

Beyond serving as a selection guide, the information included with each entry will aid you in the care of your houseplant throughout its life. Every entry will give you valuable information about how to grow your plant successfully.

The entries within each section are organized alphabetically according to botanical names. Common names are listed beneath the botancal. Should you know only the common name of a plant, you can find the botanical counterpart in the index on pages 94 to 96.

The soil recommendations for each plant listed in this encyclopedia are the all-purpose mix, the African violet mix, and the cactus mix. Instructions for making each of these are found in Chapter 2 on page 18. All temperatures are given in Fahrenheit.

African violets (Saintpaulia) are America's most popular flowering houseplant. Here, the blue and white violets accentuate the colors in the vases and lamp to create a striking yet simple tabletop arrangement.

Tuberous begonias, the type that are usually grown outdoors, will give a lovely display of blossoms if grown in abundant bright light. This plant thrives under a large skylight.

Bromeliads

Many people have discovered that bromeliads, with their exotic foliage and showy flowers, actually are not difficult to grow in an indoor environment. The most distinctive feature of the group is the rosette of leaves that mold into a cup to hold the water that nourishes the plant. From the center of some varieties, flowers and large colorful bracts emerge to create a spectacular display. These bracts are modified leaves that grow from the same axils as the flowers. Originally from the jungle, most Bromeliads are epiphytes (air plants). Like orchids, in their native habitat they grow suspended in trees and on rocks, gathering moisture and food from rainfall and debris in the air.

In your home, display them in pots or hanging baskets, or attached to boards. If you decide to keep them in pots use a light soil that can drain easily.

Overpotting and overwatering can be fatal to the small root system of these epiphytes. Just as rainfall would collect in a bromeliad, when you water, pour into the rosette's cup rather than into the soil. Bromeliads need lots of sun and high temperatures in order to bloom. If you're having trouble inducing your plant to bloom, place it in a plastic bag with a ripe apple for a few days. The ethylene gas from the apple will initiate flower buds. After the plant finishes flowering the rosette enters into a slow dying process that can last as long as 3 years. Planting the offsets that form at the base of the plant will keep your collection blooming year after year.

There are over 2,000 different species to grow. Some bromeliads are grown for their flowers, others mainly for their foliage. The following are the best to include in your indoor garden.

Aechmea species
Living vase plant

The upright rosette of thick, silver banded leaves distinguishes the striking *Aechmea chantinii*. The flowers last for several months. The most common of this group is *A. fasciata*, the urn plant. Its broad, thick leaves are mottled with stripes of gray and deep sea green. And when the conical rosette of pink bracts and large blue flowers graces the plant, a splendid effect is achieved. *A. fulgens discolor*, commonly known as the coralberry, features broad leaves, green on top and purple underneath. The contrast in the foliage is heightened by the purple flower. Red berries form after the flower dies.

Ananas species
Pineapple

If you know what a pineapple is then you know an ananas. Pineapples are the fruit of *Ananas comosus*. You can grow one by simply cutting off a bit of the fruit along with the fruit's tuft, planting it in soil (it's a terrestrial bromeliad), and placing it in full sun. Narrow, gray-green leaves with prickly ribbing running up the sides form a striking rosette; the pineapple fruit will spring from the center for an unusual display, but this will only happen after several years. *A. comosus variegatus*, commonly known as the ivory pineapple, is thought to have much more attractive foliage.

bergia species

Neorgelia species

Cryptanthus species

Vriesia species

Billbergia species
Vase plant

These are among the easiest bromeliads to grow, but they flower for only a short time. *Billbergia nutans,* known as queen's tears, has grasslike gray-green leaves. Amidst the foliage is an arching spray of pink and green flowers. Another type, *B. windii,* sports long green straplike leaves. Large bracts and pale green flowers tinged with blue cascade from this plant.

Cryptanthus species
Earth stars

Most often called earth stars because of the shape of the rosettes, their small size and great variation in leaf color make these plants good for smaller spaces or dish gardens.
   C. acaulis (starfish plant) has small, wavy edged leaves of varying shades of yellow and

green. *C. bromelioides tricolor,* the rainbow star, displays a colorful array of stripes down the length of its wavy leaves. *C. zonatus* (zebra plant) resembles zebra skin, banded in ivory and tannish brown.

Neoregelia species

These produce some of the largest rosettes composed of thick, shiny leaves. When mature, *N. carolinae tricolor* (blushing bromeliad) reaches a diameter of 30 inches. Large sawtoothed leaves, variegated in cream and green, jut out in an orderly arrangement. The plant lives up to its name, the blushing bromeliad, when, just before flowering, the youngest leaves at the base turn bright red. *N. spectabilis* features green leaves with pink-tipped ends; hence its common name, the painted fingernail plant.

Vriesia species

This genus features many plants attractive for both their foliage and flowers. *Vriesia splendens,* a popular variety, forms a rosette of wide, purple banded leaves. The common name, flaming sword, refers to its flower, a long spike of red bracts and yellow flowers. The bloom will last for several weeks.

Care of Bromeliads

Temperature:
Average constant temperatures of 65 to 70° are fine for foliage types and plants in flower. Warmer temperatures, 75 to 80°, are needed to initiate buds.

Water:
Always keep the cup of epiphytic types filled with water, preferably rain water, and change it occasionally. Allow soil to dry, then water enough to keep it barely moist. Overwatering and poor drainage will

kill the plant. Fertilize every 2 weeks.

Light:
Abundant light. An east or west-facing window is best. *Ananus* and *Cryptanthus* require full sun.

Propagation:
Remove mature offsets and a good section of roots from larger plants and pot shallowly in light soil. Keep warm.

Soil Mix:
All-purpose mix or 1 part osmunda fiber, 1 part peat moss or leaf mold, and 1 part coarse sand.

Repotting:
Rarely necessary.

Pests and Problems:
Brown areas on leaves indicate sunburn. Move plant out of direct sunlight.
   Brown tips on leaves result from dry air.
   Scale and mealybugs can be a problem.

Cephalocereus senilis

Gymnocalycium denudatum

Echinopsis species

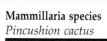
Mammillaria bocasana 'Inermis'

Cacti

Cactus is the name of a large family of over 2,000 plants, all of which are succulent. It is not true, though sometimes said, that spines are the distinguishing characteristic between cacti and other succulents. While most cacti have spines, some do not. However, they are distinguishable from other succulents by areoles, the small sunken or raised spots on their stems from which spines, flowers, and leaves emerge and grow. There are hundreds of different kinds of cacti. Below we feature a few of the best. Consult Ortho's *The World of Cactus and Succulents* for a more complete guide.

Desert cacti are extremely tolerant plants, however there is no need to impose stringent conditions on them. Cacti need a highly porous soil that drains well. Although cacti enjoy relatively dry soil, they should be watered occasionally and fed every 2 weeks with a low nitrogen fertilizer during their growing season, from early spring to midautumn. Place in a sunny window with warm daytime temperatures. At night, just like in the desert, the temperature should drop 10 to 15°.

Cephalocereus senilis
Old man cactus

This upright cylindrical cactus can reach a height of 10 feet and a diameter of 8 to 10 inches. Its gray-green body develops soft, hairy spines while still immature. Rose colored, funnelform flowers are borne on the top of the cactus after the plant is several years old. Slow growing, it is a good window sill specimen when young.

Echinopsis species
Urchin cactus

Gray-green globular to oval stems that grow singly or in clusters characterize the genus *Echinopsis*. They are distinctly ribbed, and have clusters of spines along the ribs. This cactus is best known for its long-lasting large, funnelform flowers. They range from white to pink and sometimes reach 8 inches long. This small-growing, free-flowering species makes a good window sill specimen.

Gymnocalycium denudatum
Spider cactus

The globular stems of *Gymnocalycium* grow in clusters or singly, each stem measuring 8 to 12 inches thick, depending on the species. The spider cactus features yellowish, needle shaped spines. The white to pale rose, bell shaped flowers are borne near the top of the plant in spring and summer.

Mammillaria species
Pincushion cactus

The numerous and extremely diverse members of the genus *Mammillaria* grow in globular to cylindrical forms. Specimen sizes can range from tiny individual heads only a few inches wide to massive clumps. Unlike other cacti whose flowers are borne on areoles, *Mammillaria* blooms arise from the joints of tubercles in a ring around the top of the plant. Blossoming occurs from March to October.

M. bocasana 'Inermis', the snowball cactus, displays many hooked yellowish spines and complementary yellow, bell shaped flowers.

M. prolifera is a small globe shaped cactus with bristly white spines and yellow flowers. It is commonly called

untia microdasys

Rhipsalis species

Adiantum species

little candles or silver cluster cactus.

M. zeilmanniana, the rose pincushion, is composed of a solitary stem topped with purple flowers.

Opuntia species

Two basic growth habits, broad and flat, or cylindrical, characterize this species. Small tufts of spines create a dotted pattern over the surface of the plant. *O. microdasys,* called bunny ears, has flat pads growing out of the top of larger mature pads, creating the very look that gave it its name. Bunny ears are fascinating to watch as they develop, and require very little care once established.

Rhipsalis species
Chain cactus

The jointed, branching, leafless stems of the chain cactus cascade or climb in their native habitat, making this cactus particularly well suited to hanging pots and baskets.

These epiphytes have aerial roots in their flattened or cylindrical green stems. Flower shape, color, and size vary greatly within the genus.

Care of Cacti
Temperature:
80° days; 65° nights. Winters 55 to 60°.

Water:
Water when soil is dry an inch below the surface. During winter water sparingly. Do not allow roots to stand in water; they will rot.

Light:
Ample, bright light. Place on a window sill.

Propagation:
Easily done by seed, division, or cuttings. Sow fresh seed in well aerated soil. Place in a warm, moist environment. For cuttings, follow procedure outlined in Succulents-Propagation on page 93.

Soil Mix:
Cactus mix or 2 parts loam, 2 parts sand, 1 part leaf mold.

Repotting:
Handle plant with extreme care. Wear leather gloves for protection. Wrap and tape the top of the plant in newspaper before handling.

Pests and Problems:
Root or stem rot comes from poor drainage or poor air circulation. Cool, moist conditions may also contribute.

Ferns
Although ferns lack flowers, the delicate composition of their flowering fronds instills a room with a peaceful air any flower would have trouble duplicating. This refined plant is probably the oldest houseplant on the evolutionary timeline; only the algae and the mosses come earlier. Ferns come in a multitude of shapes and sizes, from the small ones like ribbon fern, with its ribbonlike leaves, to the large, intricate fronds of maidenhair fern. Several types grouped together in entryways, patios, or conservatories can create a stunning design. They also work well displayed singly in pots or hanging baskets.

The secret of success growing ferns lies in your ability to match as nearly as possible their natural growing environment. The better you can imitate the moist, cool air and light shade of a tropical forest, the happier your fern will be. To do this will require regular attention to your plant's needs. Since their natural home is in dappled brightness, it's best to avoid exposing them to the direct sunlight that strikes a window sill. Hot, dry air spells real trouble to ferns. The air as well as the soil must always be kept moist. Provide humidity by placing the pot on a humidifying tray or in a larger pot of moist peat moss. Most ferns will grow well in average temperatures during the day with a drop at night.

The world of ferns is enormous. Of the 2,000 species to choose from, the following are some of the best types to grow indoors.

Adiantum species
Maidenhair fern

The maidenhair ferns, with their slender stems and delicate fronds, are especially attractive in groupings. They require ample light and humidity in order to survive indoors.

Asplenium nidus

Blechnum gibbum

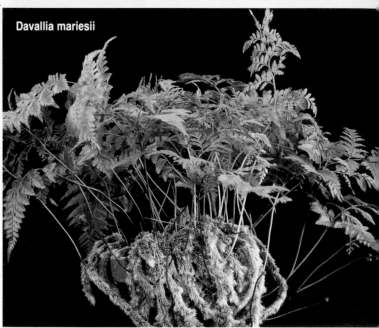

Davallia mariesii

Asplenium nedus
Bird's nest fern

This fern is well known because of its unusual fronds: The wavy, lance shaped leaves, bright green in color, are undivided and grow to be 3 feet long.

Blechnum gibbum
Lomaria

The stiff, erect fronds of this fern form a tight palmlike crown. With age the plant develops a trunk.

Davallia mariesii
Squirrel's foot fern; Ball fern

The squirrel's foot fern features wiry 10-inch stems of small fronds with leaflets. It is an excellent plant for a hanging basket.

Nephrolepis exaltata
Sword fern

Perfect for indoors in pots or hanging baskets, the long, swordlike fronds of this plant stand erect and can grow up to 3 feet long. There are several other varieties: *N.e.* 'Bostoniensis', the Boston fern, arches more so it hangs especially well. 'Fluffy Ruffles' has ruffled leaf edges; 'Whitmunii' has lacy leaf edges.

Pellaea rotundifolia
Button fern

This small fern derives its common name from its round, leathery leaflets that look like buttons. The frond's growth pattern is more horizontal than erect.

Platycerium bifurcatum
Staghorn fern

The staghorn fern grows best attached to pieces of bark or other porous material because it's an epiphyte or air plant. The broad, lancelike fronds divide about in the middle of their 2-foot length and the ends take on the appearance of stag antlers. Never allow this plant to dry out.

Polypodium aureum
Polypody fern

This tolerant, low-growing fern has rusty brown, scaly creeping rhizomes and wiry stems. It adds an unusual flair to any fern collection. The bold, straplike leathery leaves contrast sharply with the delicacy of many ferns. *P. aureum* consists of many deeply cut ruffled leaflets. The fronds can grow 2 to 5 feet long and are blue-green above and whitish beneath. This plant does well in a hanging basket.

Pteris cretica
Ribbon fern; Brake fern

Long, straplike leaves divide at the tips on this fern. Some forms are variegated, with narrow or crested leaves. The variety 'Wimsettii' is light green in color and the mature form has forked leaftips that become dense and frilly.

These ferns are easy to grow and look best when displayed in dish gardens or small pots.

Nephrolepis exaltata 'Bostoniensis'

Platycerium bifurcatum

Pellaea rotundifolia

Phlebodium aureum

Care of Ferns

Temperature:
Average 60 to 70° days; cooler nights. Minimum temperature of 50 to 55°.

Water:
Soil must be kept moist but not wet. Never allow soil to dry out. Reduce watering during winter.

Light:
Bright indirect light. An east or north window is ideal but almost any location protected from direct sun will do.

Humidity:
Moist air is essential. Use a humidifying tray.

Propagation:
It's easiest to divide large clumps or detach offsets and cultivate. Spores can be collected from the underside of fronds. When ripe they will shake off easily. Sow dry spores in sterilized soil in a sterile pot. Cover with glass and place in the shade. See page 50 for additional spore germinating methods.

Soil Mix:
All-purpose mix.

Repotting:
Necessary once a year before growing season. If roots do not fill the pot and repotting is unnecessary simply remove an inch or two of soil and add fresh soil.

Grooming:
Remove old or discolored fronds promptly. Remove any moss that grows on pot or soil surface. Loosen topsoil so air can circulate.

Pteris cretica

Flowering Houseplants

Abutilon species
Flowering maple

This tropical viny shrub of the Hollyhock family is extremely vigorous, easily growing several feet in a year. The flowers have striking rocketlike shapes, and the maple shaped leaves are sometimes dappled with yellow or white. Stems are most attractive espaliered or trained.

Abutilon's increasing popularity has spurred the development of several hybrids that produce larger blossoms in a wider range of colors. *A. hybridum* (Chinese lantern) produces white, yellow, salmon, or purple blooms. *A. megapotamicum* 'Variegata' (trailing abutilon) features red and yellow blossoms with large, dark brown, pollen-bearing anthers. *A. pictum* 'Thompsonii' bears an orange-salmon flower.

With bright direct light and moist soil this plant should grow rapidly and blossom most of the year. Fertilize monthly. Because the plant grows so rapidly, pruning is a must for retaining shape and size. Prune during the slow growth period in winter.

Temperature:
68 to 72° days; 50 to 60° nights.

Water:
Keep soil moist. Due to rapid growth, frequent thorough watering is necessary.

Light:
Bright direct sunlight at least 4 hours a day. Preferably near a south or west-facing window.

Propagation:
Cuttings root easily in spring.

Soil Mix:
All-purpose mix or 2 parts loam, 1 part peat moss, and 1 part coarse sand.

Grooming:
In winter, prune plant back to keep it 18 to 30 inches high. New shoots should appear in March.

Abutilon hybridum

Aeschynanthus species

Aeschynanthus species
Lipstick plant

This plant is most spectacular suspended at eye level so its trailing stems will show off their bright flowers. Put several plants together in one basket for a more striking effect. *A. longiflorus* features masses of deep red tubular flowers. *A. pulcher* has light green waxy leaves and scarlet flowers with yellow throats. *A. speciosus* develops orange blossoms with rust colored edges.

These trailers need warmth and shade to do well under ordinary room conditions. Place in a bright spot away from direct sunshine and water regularly from spring to autumn. During the winter allow the plant to rest in a cool, dry spot. These plants prefer a high level of humidity.

Temperature:
68 to 72° days and 65 to 68° nights. 60° in winter.

Water:
Keep soil evenly moist during growing season. Water sparingly in winter. Use tepid water: Cold water will create ring spots if it drips on the leaves.

Light:
Bright indirect light.

Propagation:
Take stem cuttings in spring or summer. Apply bottom heat to speed rooting.

Soil Mix:
African violet mix is best.

Repotting:
Repot every 2 to 3 years in the spring.

Grooming:
After flowering ceases prune back stems.

Allium schoenoprasum

Allium schoenoprasum
Chives

In summer, chives will brighten your kitchen window with beautiful clusters of rose purple flowers atop 1 to 1½–foot–tall stalks. Their foliage is attractive year round indoors and the clumps of grasslike leaves add a subtle onion flavor to salads and cooked foods.

Place on a sunny window sill with a southern exposure, keep soil moist, and fertilize every other week with a mild houseplant fertilizer. Cut shoots as needed for use in cooking. In winter, set chives outdoors in a cool spot for a few weeks to force new growth.

Temperature:
68 to 75° days; 55 to 65° nights.

Water:
Water soil when dry to the touch.

Light:
Full sun from southern exposure.

Propagation:
By seedlings, division, or dried bulbs of garlic purchased in stores. In fall or winter, break apart the cloves and plant with pointed tip up. The garlic will be ready to harvest in 8 months, after the leaves die.

Soil Mix:
All-purpose mix or 1 part loam, 1 part coarse sand, 1 part aged manure.

Grooming:
Remove flowering stems and trim plant to keep within pot.

Aphelandra squarrosa

Aphelandra squarrosa
Zebra plant

For 6 weeks in the fall this favorite of Victorian conservatories provides an impressive, orderly display of color. Large conelike, deep yellow flowers emerge from golden bracts. The rest of the year the small, erect, evergreen shrub features attractive, unusual foliage. Shiny, nearly black elliptical leaves striped with ivory veins create a zebra effect. The variety 'Louisae' is most popular. 'Apollo White', 'Dania', and 'Brockfield' are more compact and produce leaves with the most striking vein patterns.

Aphelandras tend to become gangly. To combat this, cut back after flowering, letting 1 or 2 pairs of leaves remain. Feed every 2 weeks, never allow the rootball to dry out, and keep the plant warm in winter. This plant needs a high level of humidity and will do best if placed on a humidifying tray.

Temperature:
70 to 75° days; 60 to 70° nights.

Water:
Water regularly. Soil ball should never dry out. Plant needs less water in winter.

Light:
Indirect light or filtered sun near a curtained window; eastern or western exposure.

Propagation:
In spring, cut off a side shoot that has roots and plant in 2 parts peat moss and 1 part sand.

Apply bottom heat, 65 to 75°, until new growth begins.

Soil Mix:
All-purpose soil mix.

Grooming:
In spring, cut back stem, leaving 1 or 2 pairs of healthy leaves.

Pests and Problems:
Leaf drop usually results from dry roots. Cold air or direct sun can also cause leaf drop. Low humidity causes brown leaf tips.

Azalea species

For winter color indoors it's hard to outdo Indian azaleas. Masses of white, pink, or red single or double flowers cover the dark evergreen foliage. When not in flower they make beautiful foliage plants.

Select plants that are covered with buds just about to open. To keep your plant blooming for several weeks, place it in a cool, brightly lit spot and keep the soil very moist. This plant needs an acid soil.

Temperature:
Cool, 45 to 60°.

Water:
Soil should be kept moist.

Light:
Bright indirect light. An eastern or western exposure is best.

Propagation:
After flowering, when new foliage reaches maturity, root cuttings 2 to 3 inches long from stem tips.

Soil Mix:
Well drained and acidic: 1 part sphagnum peat moss and 1 part coarse builder's sand.

Grooming:
Don't discard these plants after they bloom. Snip off dead blossoms and old leaves, trim back branches, and repot in a 1-inch larger pot. Move outside in late spring to a shady spot.

Azalea species

Begonia semperflorens

Begonia species

With over 1,500 known species, this plant family offers the indoor gardener a vast array of beauty that's easily adapted to almost any indoor environment. The different foliage shapes and colors, as well as the numbers of varieties readily available, are the distinguishing features of this group. Many varieties are grown primarily for the appearance of their foliage. See foliage section page 75. Here we discuss the best flowering varieties.

B. coccinea, angel-wing begonias, combine beautiful foliage with clusters of blooms in pink, red, orange, or white. They grow atop bamboolike stems swollen at the joints. Kusler hybrids sold by begonia specialists are some of the best types of angel-wing begonias.

The common wax or annual begonias, *B. haageana* and *B. semperflorens,* have fine, fibrous root systems which send up crisp, fleshy stems topped with waxy rounded leaves and white, red, and pink flowers.

"Semperflorens" means everblooming, so you can expect to see these blooms year round. They make excellent hanging baskets or window sill plants. Choose from varieties with single, semidouble, or fully double flowers.

Many other types of begonias are available; for more information consult your nursery or garden center.

With a minimum of trouble you should be able to keep your begonias healthy and blooming. Plenty of bright light, a normal indoor temperature that drops slightly at night, and application of fertilizer every 2 to 3 weeks are the keys to constant blooms. Begonias are very sensitive to overwatering so take care to use welldraining soil.

Temperature:
65° or above. Night temperature should drop about 5°.

Water:
Water when soil is dry to the touch.

Light:
Partial sun or good reflected light. An east or west exposure.

Propagation:
From seed, stem, and leaf cuttings, or division of the rhizome.

Soil Mix:
African violet mix or 1 part peat moss, 2 parts sphagnum moss, and 1 part perlite.

Repotting:
Plant will bloom better when potbound, so only repot it when growth is inhibited.

Grooming:
Pinch back young plants to prevent legginess and strengthen blossoms.

Camellia species

In spring these evergreen shrubs with dark green glossy leaves produce large, fragrant flowers in shades of white, pink, or red. *C. japonica*, a species commonly grown indoors, has over 2,000 known cultivars that come in a tremendous variety of colors, sizes, and shapes.

Great care must be taken to grow this plant well. It is essential to provide the proper environment. A cool room with good air circulation is a must. In the spring, a mass of buds will appear. At this point do not move the plant, and guard against fluctuations in temperature and soil moisture, or the buds will drop.

Temperature:
Days 60 to 65°; nights 40 to 45°.

Water:
These plants need plenty of water and humidity. Keep soil moist.

Light:
Bright, filtered light; eastern, western, or southern exposure.

Propagation:
By layering or stem cuttings in summer.

Soil Mix:
All-purpose mix.

Grooming:
For larger flowers, remove all but one large bud from a cluster for every 2 to 4 inches of

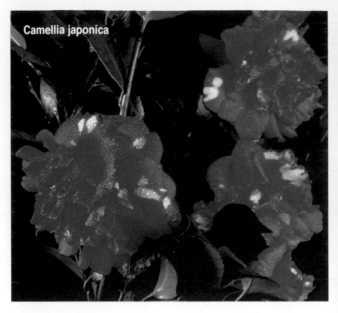
Camellia japonica

branch. Prune back after flowering.

Pests and Problems:
Improper temperature and watering will cause buds to drop. Provide good drainage so harmful salts cannot accumulate.

Chrysanthemum morifolium
Florist's mum

These plants are greenhouse hybrids that are often given as gifts. They are considered to be houseplants because they are most often purchased to be displayed in the home while blooming. They can be transplanted in the garden but are difficult to grow outdoors. Think of florist's mums as cut flowers that last longer.

Commercial growers apply dwarfing chemicals and place the plants in the dark to give them short days and long nights in order to induce them to flower by a certain date. The small plants with large flowers of every color except blue are available throughout the year.

Avoid buying large, leafy plants that have no buds. Instead, look for plants with a few open blossoms and lots of buds. Place the plant in a cool room on a window sill

Chrysanthemum morifolium

where it will receive about 4 hours of direct sun daily. Morning or evening sun is best. It should bloom for 6 to 8 weeks.

If you want to save the plant, prune it back and reduce watering, then plant it in your garden. Without the aid of growth retardants they tend to become quite leggy. Pinch back often to maintain a full, bushy plant.

Temperature:
60 to 65° days; 45 to 50° nights.

Water:
Keep soil moist. Plant tends to dry out quickly.

Light:
Direct sun in morning and at dusk. Bright light is essential.

Propagation:
Take stem tip cuttings of new shoots in spring.

Soil Mix:
All-purpose mix.

Grooming:
For sturdy plants with big flowers, pinch back frequently before buds appear. After blooming cut stems back to 3 inches.

Pests and Problems:
Leaves wilt if soil dries out. High temperatures cause flowers to develop rapidly and die quickly. Often buds that fail to open did not receive enough light.

Clivia miniata

Clivia miniata
Kafir lily

This herbaceous plant is a member of the amaryllis family and is named after Charlotte Clive, Duchess of Northumberland, who developed it as an indoor plant in 1866. Thick stems 12 to 15 inches long emerge from a surround of leathery straplike leaves to support large clusters of orange, trumpet shaped flowers with yellow throats. French and Belgian hybrids come in yellow to deep red-orange. After flowers fade in late spring, ornamental red berries form to add a touch of lasting color.

This winter bloomer will

Columnea species

Cyclamen persicum

do well in a room that receives plenty of indirect sunlight and also cools down overnight. Houses in cold climates have little trouble accommodating this need. Crowded roots left undisturbed for years produce the best blooms; repotting is rarely necessary. During the fall the plant rests: Apply no fertilizer and reduce water. From January to August fertilize once a month.

Temperature:
68 to 72° days; 50 to 55° nights. Minimum winter temperature of 45°.

Water:
Water frequently during flowering. After flowering allow soil to dry out between watering.

Light:
Ample indirect light. Curtain-filtered light is best.

Propagation:
In late spring divide bulbs.

Soil Mix:
Commercial potting soil.

Repotting:
Only every 3 to 4 years. Soil can wash out of the pot due to heavy watering. If the soil level is lowered in this way, add new soil to the top of the pot.

Columnea species

There are some 150 different species of this member of the Gesneriad family. They come from Central and South America and the West Indies, and their natural habitat is the damp tropical forest. They make wonderful container plants, and because they are semiupright or trailing plants, they look especially nice in hanging baskets. The brightly colored tubular flowers come in orange, scarlet, and yellow and will bloom all through the winter. Flowers range in size from ½ inch to 4 inches depending on the variety. Leaves vary from tiny, button size to 3 inches in length.

   C. banksii, which has waxy leaves, is one of the easiest to grow. *C. gloriosa* has hairy leaves and red flowers.

   These aren't the easiest plants to grow but keeping the air moist will help them stay healthy and blooming. During the winter water carefully and keep them away from heat sources.

Temperature:
70° days; 65° nights, cooler in winter.

Water:
Soil should be kept moist. Reduce watering in winter.

Light:
Bright indirect light.

Propagation:
Take stem cuttings after flowering. Apply bottom heat.

Soil Mix:
All-purpose mix.

Repotting:
Repot in late spring every 2 to 3 years.

Grooming:
As soon as flowering ceases, cut back stems.

Cyclamen species
Cyclamen; Shooting star

Heart shaped, dark green leaves surround upright stems topped with butterflylike blossoms from midautumn until midspring. Of the 15 species in the genus, *C. persicum* is most commonly grown indoors and readily available through florists. It's best to purchase your plants in early fall when the blooming season begins.

   This plant prefers a cool room with good air circulation but no drafts. When blooming, it needs as much sun as possible. Fertilize every 2 weeks.

   Many people automatically discard cyclamen after blooming, but they can be kept if they are given special care. After blooming ceases and foliage dies down, keep the tuber in a cool spot and let the soil dry. In midsummer repot with new soil in a small pot and place it in a warm spot to encourage good root growth. As the plant grows, gradually return it to a cool climate (55°) to induce blooming.

Temperature:
60 to 65° days; nights 60° or lower, 40 to 50° is ideal.

Water:
Keep soil moist.

Light:
Bright reflected light or a curtain-filtered southern or western exposure is best.

Propagation:
From seeds in early spring. *C. persicum* strains bloom only after 15 to 18 months.

Soil Mix:
African violet mix or 2 parts peat moss, 1 part packaged potting soil, and 1 part sharp sand or perlite.

Repotting:
The beetlike tuber should be replanted to the same depth it had been planted previously. About half of it will show above the soil level. Set the pot outside and keep soil barely moist for the remainder of the summer.

Episcia species

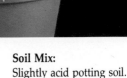
Euphorbia pulcherrima

Episcia species

This relative of the African violet makes a striking hanging plant. Like strawberries, it has runners or stolons, which cascade down the sides of the pot.

E. cupreata (flame violet) has small, reddish orange, tubular flowers among erect leaves that are copper colored with silver veins. E. dianthiflora (lace flower) has white frilled flowers and velvet, dark green leaves. These summer bloomers make attractive foliage plants the rest of the year. Grouping several different varieties together in one pot creates an intriguing arrangement.

One reason these plants have not achieved the wide popularity enjoyed by the African violets is because they need lots of moisture in the air. This is somewhat difficult to provide if you want to display them in the most flattering manner, by hanging them. To provide the moisture needed, surround the base of the plant with damp peat. Runners will root easily in surrounding compost to form plantlets. After flowering, pinch back stems to induce branching.

Temperature:
Average warmth, 75° days, 65 to 70° nights; not less than 55° in winter.

Water:
Moist at all times during growing season. Reduce amount in winter.

Light:
No direct sun, just bright light. Plants need at least 14 to 16 hours of bright indirect light or artificial light a day.

Propagation:
Layer runners in compost; they will root and form plantlets.

Soil Mix:
African violet mix or 2 parts peat moss, 1 part packaged potting soil, and 1 part sharp sand or perlite.

Repotting:
Every year in spring.

Grooming:
Pinch off the tips of the stems to encourage branching. For fresh growth cut back the plant when it has stopped blooming.

Euphorbia pulcherrima
Poinsettia

The poinsettia was first found in the 1800s growing as a wildflower in Mexico, and since has been cultivated in the United States to become the most popular live Christmas gift given today. The large white, pink, or red flower is actually a group of bracts which surround a small, inconspicuous true flower. Ranging in height from 1 to 3 feet, some have blossoms that stretch 6 to 12 inches across.

With proper care these plants will continue to bloom for several months and some can be made to blossom the following season. While blooming the plants simply need plenty of sun and protection from drafts and sudden changes in temperature. Reduce water during the rest period from spring to midsummer, then increase waterings and apply fertilizer every 2 weeks. These plants normally flower in the fall when the nights are long. Beginning about October 1, they need 2 weeks of long (12-hour) nights, uninterrupted by any light source before flowers are initiated. If your plant is indoors, be sure that household lights do not interrupt this darkness requirement. You may have to place the plant in a dark closet at night or put it outdoors in a protected spot. (See page 42–43.)

Temperature:
68° or above days; 50 to 65° nights.

Water:
Allow soil to dry somewhat, then water thoroughly. Reduce amount during rest period.

Light:
Place in a sunny window where plants will receive plenty of light. A western or southern exposure is best. In summer this location may become too hot; if so, move the plant farther from the window or protect it with curtains during the heat of the day.

Propagation:
Root cuttings of tips of new growth in summer.

Soil Mix:
Slightly acid potting soil.

Grooming:
Thin out branches in summer to produce larger bracts the next season. Pinching back will make the plant bushier but also may reduce the size of the bracts.

Fuchsia hybrida
Fuchsia; Lady's eardrops

The showy, simple flowers and thin green or variegated leaves of fuchsia form beautiful shrubs. Sepals are petallike structures that enclose flower buds. Normally they are green however fuchsias have colored sepals that flare open to reveal pendant petals. The petals are either the same color as the sepals or another hue. Colors range from white through pink, red, lavender, violet, and purple in countless combinations. There are thousands of fuchsia strains that come in a great variety of shapes and sizes. Many make excellent hanging plants or do well in window boxes.

Fuchsias thrive only in cool summer environments. Success largely depends on finding the proper spot, so choose your location carefully. During the summer it's a good idea to plant or move them outdoors. Feed frequently and always keep the soil moist. Hanging basket plants dry out quickly so check them frequently.

hsia hybrida

Gardenia jasminoides

Temperature:
Cool, 65 to 70° days; 60 to 65° nights.

Water:
Keep soil damp, but do not allow roots to stand in water.

Light:
Bright indirect light. Partial shade is good.

Propagation:
Root 2 to 3-inch cuttings of soft green wood in potting soil mixed with equal amounts of vermiculite. Do not keep the new cuttings too warm.

Soil Mix:
African violet mix, all-purpose mix, or 3 parts leaf mold, 1 part humus, and 1 part sand. Provide good drainage.

Grooming:
For a bushier plant pinch back 3 or more times in the spring.

Gardenia jasminoides
Gardenia; Cape jasmine

Discovered in China around 1763, there are about 200 species of this flower. The heady aroma of these creamy, spiraling blossoms is sure to please everyone. G. jasminoides has large, glossy, dark green leaves and produces an abundance of flowers. It is the type most often grown indoors. Some varieties bloom in the summer, while others bloom throughout the year. Oil extracted from the flowers is used in perfumes and tea. They make excellent cut flowers.

Formerly, these plants were very popular additions to the greenhouse, and rightly so. Gardenias kept indoors must have high humidity and cool nights along with plenty of

sunlight. The plant will not set buds if night temperatures exceed 65°.

Temperature:
68 to 72° days; 60 to 65° nights.

Water:
Soil should be moist and well drained.

Light:
Keep in full sun with partial shade during midday.

Propagation:
Take stem cuttings and root them in vermiculite. Cover with glass or clear plastic to prevent moisture loss, and apply bottom heat.

Soil Mix:
All-purpose mix.

Grooming:
To get flowers in midwinter, pinch buds off until late September.

Pests and Problems:
Bud drop results from any stress, especially low humidity. Set plants on a humidifying tray.

Hippeastrum
Amaryllis; Barbados lily

The strap shaped leaves of this lilylike flower emerge after the plant blooms. One- to two-foot stems sport clusters of 3 or 4 flowers 8 to 10 inches across. They come in a wide array of colors: 'Apple Blossom' is bluish pink; 'Beautiful Lady' is salmon orange; 'Fire Dance' is bright red, and 'Scarlet Ad-

Hippeastrum species

miral' is deep scarlet. Seed-grown bulbs are sold by color in stores. Named strains available through mail order firms tend to produce more robust flowers.

The plant blooms in late winter and is moderately easy to grow; with proper care it can last for many years. Pot prepared bulbs as early as October. When flower spike appears place in well-lit cool (60°) location. As buds grow and eventually flower keep moist and fertilize monthly. After flowering the foliage will die back; allow the plant to dry up and become dormant.

Temperature:
65 to 70° days, 60 to 65° nights. Keep plants cooler while they are blooming.

Water:
Keep moist during flowering.

Light:
Bright light. A southern or eastern exposure is best.

Propagation:
Small offset bulbs develop alongside the large ones. These can be planted after the main bulb is through flowering. It takes seeds 3 to 4 years to produce flowering plants.

Soil Mix:
All-purpose mix.

Repotting:
Every 3 to 4 years. Place the bulb in a pot with a diameter that allows a 2-inch ring of soil around the bulb. Water well once, then wait for plant to emerge.

Grooming:
After flowering, do not remove foliage from the bulb until it has died back. This gives the leaves a chance to make food for storage in the bulb.

Hydrangea macrophylla

Impatiens species

Cattleya orchid

Hydrangea macrophylla
Common big leaf hydrangea

These large flowers can be purchased in bloom during the spring or summer. Round clusters 8 to 10 inches in diameter are composed of 1 to 1½-inch flowers. Shiny oval leaves 2 to 6 inches long set off the clusters. Flowers are pink, red, white, blue, or mauve. Blue flowers will turn pink in neutral or alkaline soil. Aluminum sulfate or iron sulfate added to the soil will produce blue flowers; applications of lime or wood ashes will neutralize the soil pH and produce flowers in the pink to red range.

The plant is easy to care for while flowering but will not usually bloom in the home the following season. For blooms to last 6 weeks, two conditions must be met. Place the plant in a cool location and never allow the soil to dry. Daily watering may be necessary during flowering. If your tap water is very hard be sure to leach the soil frequently and use rain water whenever possible. In mild climates you can plant it outdoors for summer blooms.

Temperature:
68 to 72° days, 50 to 60° nights.

Water:
Soil should be well drained and kept constantly moist.

Light:
Bright indirect light. Curtain-filtered sun in a cool spot is best.

Propagation:
Too difficult for the home grower.

Soil Mix:
All-purpose mix.

Grooming:
Cut back stems to half their height in the fall. Then replant in garden.

Impatiens species
Impatiens; Balsam

Growing impatiens is an easy way to bring natural color indoors year round. They're excellent decorations for a sunny table, window box, or window sill.

I. balsaminii (common balsam) is an annual that will easily bloom for months in summer and winter, then die. Taller varieties of this species are usually grown in the garden and although you may be tempted to bring them indoors, their larger size and lanky shape become more apparent and distracting once they are transferred indoors.

Dwarf varieties are far more attractive. Another species *I. wallerana* (busy Lizzie), an everblooming perennial, is also easy to raise indoors. These are also known as *I. holstii* and *I. sultanii* and they grow up to 15 inches high. All of these species sport flowers 1 to 2 inches across in a wide array of colors—pink, red, orange, purple, white, and some variegated. 'Tangerine' features a richly colored flower and handsome leaves.

Regular care will reward you with a constantly blossoming plant. Place in a sunny spot, keep soil moist, and feed every week. Slightly potbound plants will bloom more profusely. Pinch back leggy branches to control shape and encourage blossoms.

Temperature:
65 to 75° days and nights; not less than 55° in winter.

Water:
Water when soil is dry to the touch.

Light:
Bright light. Place near a western or eastern window. May need to supplement with artificial light, especially if blooms fail to appear.

Propagation:
From stem cuttings anytime of year.

Repotting:
Will flower most easily when slightly potbound. If necessary, repot in the spring.

Soil Mix:
African violet mix.

Grooming:
Pinch tips of plants to encourage bushiness and prevent legginess.

Orchids

Growing these exquisite, colorful flowers is regarded by most people as the supreme gardening achievement, which only experts attempt. But in fact, some species of orchids grow quite well indoors and require less routine care than other houseplants. In addition, improved breeding techniques have significantly increased the availability and lowered the cost of many species. Placed on a window sill in your living room an orchid is sure to be the center of attraction. It's always wise to purchase mature plants that are in bloom. Described below are some of the best "houseplant" orchids.

Cattleya, the large classical orchid most often seen in corsages, is good for beginners to try. The vigorous plants produce gorgeous blooms when they receive plenty of sun and average daytime temperatures.

Dendrobiums are mostly epiphytic orchids with both evergreen and deciduous types available. Large flowers bloom in clusters or in a row along the stem. They last for at least 1 week and up to several months depending on the species. These plants need plenty of sun, as do most orchids.

Oncydium, the dancing lady orchid, is a large group of epiphytic orchids. They produce stalks of yellow flowers speckled with brown. Flower size depends on the species.

Paphiopedilum, the lady slipper orchid, will produce fragrant blooms throughout the

ndrobium orchid

Paphiopedilum orchid

Pelargonium species

cydium orchid

Phalaenopsis orchid

year, if given plenty of moisture and full sun.

Phalaenopsis, commonly known as the moth orchid, unfurls sprays of 2 to 3-inch flowers in a range of colors. The plant grows up to 30 inches high. These shade-loving plants are easy to grow at temperatures of 75° in the day and 60° at night.

Care of Orchids

Temperature:
Normal daytime temperatures of 70 to 75° are fine. A night temperature 15° lower is good, but it should not dip below 55°.

Water:
Watering is of utmost importance. The needs of particular species will vary. In general, keep soil moist and always use tepid water.

Light:
Ample light. At least 10 to 15 hours a day. Protect from direct sun. Supplement with artificial light, especially in winter.

Humidity:
Lots of moisture in the air is essential. Place orchids on humidifying trays. Good air circulation is a must.

Propagation:
By division of plant. Stake new plants.

Soil Mix:
Use commercially prepared orchid mixture. Epiphytic orchids can be grown in pots of osmunda fiber or ground bark.

Repotting:
Allow roots to extend beyond the pot as long as the plant continues to grow well. When growth is inhibited, repot.

Pests and Problems:
Limp leaves or flowers are caused first by insufficient light; secondly by improper watering, most probably overwatering.

Yellowing leaves can be expected if leaves are old or plant is deciduous; otherwise, it results from overwatering or sunburn.

Brown spots are caused by too much sun or leaf spot disease.

Pelargonium species
Geranium

These natives of South Africa are versatile and appeal to most everyone. There are thousands of species and named varieties, some grown outdoors, others easily moved indoors from outside. Many add a distinctive charm to an indoor decor all year long.

Common geraniums are hybrids of *Pelargonium hortorum*, and often have a darker green or blackish ring in each leaf. Varieties are available in red, salmon, apricot, tangerine, pink, and white. They will bloom all year, but they bloom best in January and February.

Fancy leaf geraniums, *P. domesticum*, have varicolored leaves, often in bronzes, scarlets, and yellows.

Never venturing above 8 inches, dwarf geraniums have the delicate proportion and shape perfect for tables and window sills, but they are not as popular as others because they require cooler temperatures. Ivy geraniums, varieties of *P. peltatum*, bear leathery leaves with a shape similar to English ivy, and sport many clusters of showy flowers, often veined with a darker shade of the overall color. These are excellent in hanging baskets near windows.

Geraniums are easy to care for in the proper environment. A sunny window sill where it is cool (never rising above 75°) and dry is ideal. Fertilize once a week and water when the soil is dry to the touch. For bushiness and strong flowering pinch back plants in autumn, and always remove dead blossoms promptly.

Temperature:
70 to 75° days; nights cooler, not less than 45° in winter.

Water:
Water thoroughly when soil is dry below the surface. Do not overwater, especially during the winter when less is needed.

Light:
Direct sunlight for 4 hours a day is essential.

Propagation:
In summer take stem cuttings and root in moist vermiculite, uncovered.

Soil Mix:
All-purpose mix.

Grooming:
Pinch back in spring for bushiness.

Primula malacoides

Rosa hybrids

Primula species
Primrose

These winter bloomers, frequently given as gifts, make one of the best pot plants. Large, erect flowers grouped in clusters emerge above leafy rosettes from December to April.

Three species especially suited to indoors are *P. malacoides*, *P. obconica*, and *P. sinensis*. The largest is *P. malacoides*, commonly called the fairy primrose. Starlike, scented flowers are borne in tiers on tall stalks. *P. obconica* (German primrose) reaches a foot in height and blooms in white, lilac, crimson, and salmon. *P. sinensis* (Chinese primrose) is the primula usually carried by florists. This small plant features delicate, ruffled flowers in a wide range of colors, pink being the most common. All 3 primroses have similar care requirements.

A well-lit, cool area such as a sun porch is ideal because primroses like to keep their roots cool. If the plant is located near a warm, sunny window, pack coarse sphagnum moss up to the rim of the pot to help keep the soil and the roots cool. Pinch off blossoms as they fade and feed once a week with a dilute concentration of liquid fertilizer.

Temperature:
Cool, 55 to 60° range during flowering period.

Water:
Constantly moist soil. Never allow soil to dry out.

Light:
Bright indirect light.

Propagation:
Sow seeds in June or July.

Soil Mix:
All-purpose mix supplemented with lime.

Repotting:
P. obconica and *P. sinensis* can be retained for next season. Repot and place in a shaded, cool, airy location during summer. Water sparingly until autumn. Remove yellowed leaves.

Pests and Problems:
Too much heat will shorten the flowering period, as will failure to remove dead flowers. Soft or rotten crown occurs when it has been planted too deeply.

Rosa hybrids
Miniature roses

Although usually thought of as exquisite additions to outdoor gardens, miniature roses can grace your home also. Delicate 1 to 1½-inch blooms are available in a spectrum of colors. Grown as small bushes, climbers, or standards, they make an appealing indoor display. Their limited popularity stems from the difficulty gardeners have had in making them flourish indoors. However, new hybrids have eliminated many of the problems. 'Beauty Secret', 'Janna', 'Green Ice', and 'Toy Clown' are a few of the best.

In order to grow the miniatures successfully, they simply need the same care they would receive if grown outdoors. First of all, place them in a spot with abundant light and cool, well-circulated air. High humidity is a must, so place a humidifying tray beneath the pots. Allow the soil to dry slightly between thorough waterings. Apply a high nitrogen fertilizer every 2 weeks. Roses readily pick up fungus, so clean your plants meticulously: Rinse the leaves regularly with water, remove yellowing leaves, and clip off the old blossoms at once. When pests such as aphids or mites invade, treat them immediately. After the last blossoms of summer have faded, prune back your plant severely.

Temperature:
Average warmth; keep at 60 to 70° during the growing season.

Water:
Water thoroughly after soil dries slightly.

Light:
Full sun. A sunny window sill is ideal. During short-day winter months supplemental light is necessary.

Propagation:
In spring take stem cuttings.

Soil Mix:
All-purpose mix or 1 part loam, 1 part peat moss, 1 part builder's sand.

Repotting:
In autumn repot and move outdoors; bury the pot in soil. Bring indoors in January.

Grooming:
Remove old blooms to lengthen flowering season.

Saintpaulia species
African violet

In terms of popularity, these plants—originally collected in Africa in the late 19th century—are first in any list of favorite flowering plants. No other plant equals Saintpaulia in ability to thrive and bloom indoors for months on end.

Rosettes of velvety leaves on short stems surround clusters of flowers in white, shades of pink, red, violet, purple, or blue. Its compact size makes it perfect for window sills, small tabletop arrangements, and hanging displays.

There are thousands of named African violets from which to choose. For beginners, it's best to start with varieties that have plain, green leaves rather than fancier types, which are not as easy to grow. Consult local experts or plant catalogs to determine varieties you find most appealing.

Despite their reputation for being temperamental, African violets generally are not difficult to grow. The fact that millions of indoor gardeners grow and collect them attests to their beauty and ease of flowering. Plenty of bright indirect light is the key factor in achieving constant bloom. Supple-

ment with artificial light if the plant stops blooming, especially in the winter, when the plant receives less than 12 hours of good light a day. Evenly moist soil, warm temperatures, high air humidity, and feeding once a month are the other important factors for good growth. The plants will flower best with only one crown (the area where stems come together and join the roots). Use additional crown growth for rooting new plants.

Miniature African violets
Recently miniature varieties have received more attention. Potted in 2½-inch pots, they only grow to be 8 inches across and are real space savers that make wonderful additions to collections, indoor landscapes, terrariums, or miniature greenhouses. Semiminiatures have somewhat smaller leaves and crowns than standards, but their flowers grow to be almost as large. Some of the best miniatures are: 'Midget Midnight', 'Tiny Fantasy', 'Bagdad', and 'Silver Bells'. Outstanding semiminiatures include: 'Dora Baker', 'Sweet Pixie', and 'Little Dogwood'.

In addition to following the care techniques for standard African violets, here are some

valuable tips for growing miniatures: The soil must be kept constantly moist. This is especially important and difficult to do because the small amount of soil will dry out quickly. Potting several plants together in a larger pot may make your care routine a lot easier by increasing the humidity, moisture, and amount of soil and nutrients available to the plants; however, avoid crowding the plants too closely.

Temperature:
Average 72 to 75° days; 60 to 65° nights. Keep plants away from cold window panes. Sudden changes in temperature are harmful.

Water:
Keep soil evenly moist. Only use water that is at room temperature. Avoid wetting foliage: Cold water spots the leaves. Leach soil occasionally.

Light:
Bright light. Direct sun in the winter is fine but summer sun may be too strong. In general, the more light the better. During the winter, supplement with artificial light so that the plant receives at least 14 hours of light a day.

Humidity:
Provide moist air by surrounding the base of the plant with moist peat moss or placing on a humidifying tray.

Propagation:
In spring, take leaf cuttings or sow seeds.

Soil Mix:
African violet mix. For a light, porous mix combine 1 part garden loam, 1 part leaf mold, and 1 part sand.

Repotting:
African violets like being slightly potbound. A pot about half the width of the plant's spread is a good size. Plant rooted leaf cuttings in 2½-inch pots and gradually pot up.

Grooming:
Remove all dead leaves and flowers promptly, stems included. Shape the plant by removing side shoots.

Pests and Problems:
Mushy, brown blooms and buds indicate botrytis blight. Pick off diseased parts. Provide good air circulation, avoid high humidity, and reduce amount of nitrogen in fertilizer.

Yellow rings on leaf surface are caused by cold water touching foliage. Use tepid water only; cold water will spot leaves.

Streaked, misshapen leaves with irregular yellow spots are caused by a virus; there is no effective cure so plants should be discarded.

If a healthy plant wilts suddenly, it has crown rot, which results from an erratic watering routine. Do not allow the soil to dry out completely and then soak it; maintain a constant level of soil moisture.

Severe temperature changes may also cause crown rot. This is difficult to remedy. Discard the plant.

Lack of flowers is probably caused by inadequate light. Supplement daylight with artificial light. Very dry air or very cold air are also possible causes. Repotting and moving the plant to a new location can inhibit flowering for a long time.

Yellowing leaves result from dry air, too much sun, or incorrect watering. Improper fertilizing can also yellow the leaves. Follow directions closely.

Brown, brittle leaves develop from soil that is deficient in nutrients. Repot if soil is old, otherwise fertilize regularly.

Slow growth and leaves curled downward indicate that the temperature is too low.

Soft foliage and few flowers can be caused by temperatures that are too high.

Brown edged leaves and small flowers are a result of low humidity. Place plants on humidifying trays.

Schlumbergera truncata

Sinningia speciosa

Schlumbergera species
Thanksgiving cactus; Crab cactus

The unusual stems and timely blossoms of these commonly grown houseplants are both delightful and fascinating. The old favorite, *S. bridgesii* (also called *Zygocactus truncatus and Z. bridgesii*) features striking, bright green arched branches. Made up of smooth, flat, scalloped, 1½-inch-long joints, they have a drooping habit, especially when in flower. The multitrumpeted, 3-inch-long, rosy red flowers appear at Christmastime. *S. gaerneri* (also known as *Rhipsalidopsis gaertneri*) is often confused with *S. bridgesii*, but this plant droops less and the stems and joints sport scarlet, upright or horizontal, sharply tipped flowers at Eastertime, sometimes again in early fall. Cultivars in shades of pink and red are also available.

Schlumbergeras are native to the jungles of South America, where they grow on trees. As potted plants they require a rich, porous soil. Keep the soil moist, not wet, and fertilize weekly when not in rest periods. They will do well in front of a cool, bright window. During the summer you can move them outdoors into partial shade. Budding results from short days during October and November or a cold shock. To provide this, place your plants outdoors for a time during the fall.

Temperature:
Before blossoming, night temperatures of 55 to 60°; once buds set, 70 to 75° days and 60 to 70° nights.

Water:
Moist, but not soggy soil. Allow soil to dry between waterings when the plant rests.

Light:
Bright reflected light. Western or northern exposure is best.

Propagation:
From stem cuttings or seeds when not in flower. Place stem sections in moist vermiculite.

Soil Mix:
African violet mix or 1 part potting soil, 2 parts leaf mold, and 1 part perlite.

Sinningia speciosa
Gloxinia

These velvety leafed Brazilian plants are members of the Gesneriad family. In practice, growers tend to call the natural species *Sinningias*, and the hybrids *Gloxinias*. Encircled by large, stalkless leaves, bell shaped flowers with ruffled edges are borne in a cluster atop long stems. Some miniatures—both hybrids and species—have 1½-inch leaves and inch-long flowers that bloom year round.

To grow well and for many years gloxinias need humidity, full sun in the winter, and shade in the summer. Keep the soil moist, but not too wet, and be sure to use tepid water. After blooming ceases and leaf growth reaches a standstill, gradually withhold water until stems and leaves die down; put the plant in a cool, dark, mouseproof place for 2 to 4 months while the tuber rests. Water sparingly until new growth appears, then repot into fresh soil, move into light and warmth, and provide moisture. While they are growing, feed gloxinias every 2 weeks.

Temperature:
65 to 75° days; 60 to 70° nights.

Water:
Barely moist. Do not allow soil to dry out. Do not water crowns. Use tepid water.

Light:
Bright indirect light. A southern or western exposure is best.

Propagation:
From seed or leaf cuttings rooted in damp sand or perlite.

Soil Mix:
African violet mix.

Repotting:
When the plant resumes growth after rest periods, repot with new soil.

Grooming:
Handle carefully; the brittle leaves break off easily.

Pests and Problems:
Gloxinias do not bloom all year long. After blooming allow them to rest for a period of 2 to 4 months. Extra water or fertilizers at this stage will cause them to die.

Spathiphyllum species
Peace lily; Spathe flower

The distinctive flower of *Spathiphyllum* evokes a feeling for its common name, the peace lily. The spathe is a pure white bract that encloses the true flowers. Sometimes more than 4 inches wide and 6 inches long, it unfurls to form a softly curved backdrop for the central column of these closely set tiny flowers. The fragrant blossom clearly resembles its relative, anthurium. Spoon shaped leaves on long stalks surround the flower and mirror its shape.

When not in flower, *Spathiphyllum* makes a very attractive foliage plant, especially in a shady location. Choose the plants by size: *S.* 'Clevelandii' (white anthurium) grows to a height of 2 feet. *S. floribundum* (snowflower) has leaves less than a foot tall. The largest *S.* 'Mauna Loa' reaches 3 feet. They bloom in spring and sometimes in autumn. After a few days the white spathe will turn pale green.

This is one of the easiest large flowering plants to grow, especially under limited light conditions. A few hours of bright indirect light daily, normal to warm house temperatures, and regular watering and feeding is all that is needed

pathiphyllum 'Mauna Loa'

Streptocarpus species

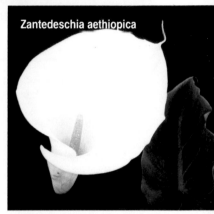

Zantedeschia aethiopica

to bring this plant to bloom. Cold drafts will harm the plant, and the surrounding air should be moist, so place the pot on a humidifying tray or fill it with moist peat moss. Wash leaves occasionally to protect the plant from scales and mites.

Temperature:
65 to 75° days; 60 to 68° nights.

Water:
During the growing period, keep well-draining soil moist. Water less frequently in winter.

Light:
Bright indirect light; this plant can survive in the shade.

Propagation:
Easily done by division or seed.

Soil Mix:
All-purpose mix with sphagnum added.

Repotting:
Best done in February or March, but usually not necessary on a yearly basis.

Streptocarpus species
Cape primrose

Commonly known as the cape primrose, *Streptocarpus* is a relative of the African violet and gloxinia and can be grown under similar conditions.

Stemless, fleshy leaves hover below trumpetlike flowers sup-

ported by stems similar to those of primroses. Many colorful varieties in white, pink, red, violet, or blue are available. *S. saxorum* has small leaves and lavender flowers. The 'Wiesmoor' hybrids reach 6 to 8 inches and bear 1½ to 2-inch flowers for 2 months. 'Nymph' hybrids grow 10 to 12 inches high with 1 to 2-inch flowers that bloom from spring to fall.

Although *Streptocarpus* can be a temperamental, erratic bloomer for many indoor gardeners, it will flourish with the correct treatment. This Gesneriad prefers a cooler environment than African violets and especially enjoys a temperature drop at night. Raise it in shallow pots with good drainage, and where the air is humid. A north-facing window away from midday sun is ideal. Feed regularly and water freely during the flowering season.

Temperature:
65 to 70° days; 60 to 65° nights.

Water:
Keep moist during growing period. Provide good drainage.

Light:
Protect from direct sun; place in a spot with plenty of indirect light. Supplement with artificial lights.

Propagation:
Easily done from leaf cuttings. Cut a leaf lengthwise along the vein. Place cut side down in

moist sand and peat. Roots and leaves of new plantlets will grow from the vein.

Soil Mix:
All-purpose mix or 2 parts peat moss, 1 part potting soil, and 1 part sharp sand or perlite.

Repotting:
Not necessary very often.

Pests and Problems:
Too little light causes leaves and flowers to droop.

Zantedeschia aethiopica
Calla lily; Florist's calla

A creamy white spathe, 5 to 10 inches in length, curves around a fragrant yellow spike to form this elegant perennial. Surrounded by wide, lance shaped, glossy leaves, the trumpetlike flowers appear atop yard-long stems in winter and spring.

Varieties come in different sizes. 'Childsiana' produces many flowers and grows to 12 inches. 'Minor' spurts to a height of 18 inches with flowers 4 inches long. 'Godfreyana', somewhat smaller than other Calla lily species, bears many flowers. Other sizes and colors are available but these species are not usually grown indoors.

These imposing plants are a joy to grow as long as all their needs can be adequately met. Plenty of growing space, light, and moist soil and air produce strong growth and abundant blossoms. Place on a

humidifying tray and feed your plant weekly with a mild houseplant fertilizer. During the summer the plant rests. Reduce water so leaves will yellow and die. Cut off dead growth and in autumn repot the rhizomes about 1 inch deep in pots. Keep cool and barely moist until new growth appears, then resume normal care.

Temperature:
60 to 70° days; 50 to 60° nights.

Water:
Water freely during the blooming season.

Light:
Place in a bright, well lit spot that receives at least 4 hours of direct sun in the morning or evening.

Propagation:
By division of offsets or rhizomes in the fall.

Soil Mix:
African violet mix.

Aglaonema commutatum

Araucaria heterophylla

Foliage Houseplants

Aglaonema commutatum
Chinese evergreen

This is regarded as a favorite in homes in the United States because it is tolerant of a wide range of conditions. The plant grows to 2 feet tall and has oblong, lance shaped leaves 6 to 9 inches long and 2 to 3 inches wide. The waxy, deep green leaves are marked with silver bars between pale lateral veins. Creamy white, waxy flowers shaped like calla lilies bloom in late summer to early fall. Tight clusters of inch-long yellowish red berries follow the flowers. This plant tolerates both poor light and dry air, so it will certainly do well in the average home. Place it in a moderately lit spot and keep soil evenly moist. Feed every 3 weeks with a mild fertilizer solution. Chinese evergreen prefers a humid environment, so place it on a humidifying tray if the air is particularly dry. Growth slows during the winter.

Temperature:
Moderate to warm: 70 to 80° days; 60 to 65° nights.

Water:
Keep soil evenly moist, drier in winter.

Light:
Moderate light; will tolerate partial shade. A north-facing window is best.

Propagation:
Root division, stem cuttings, or seeds in spring and summer.

Soil Mix:
All-purpose mix.

Repotting:
Blossoms best when potbound.

Araucaria heterophylla
Norfolk Island pine

Symmetrical tiers of branches with needlelike leaves are featured on *A. heterophylla* (also known as *A. excelsia*). Trees range in size from those small enough to be displayed in a terrarium to very tall specimens placed in entryways or large rooms.

This is an easy-to-grow conifer; nevertheless, it grows slowly, so be patient if you want it to grow into a large specimen. Place it in a brightly lit, cool location. Keep the soil moist and protect it from hot, dry air. The plant rests during the winter. With proper care, it can eventually reach 10 to 15 feet tall indoors.

Temperature:
55 to 65° days and nights. Cooler in winter.

Water:
Water regularly to keep soil moderately moist.

Light:
Bright indirect light. Protect from direct sun in summer.

Propagation:
Not recommended.

Soil Mix:
All-purpose mix.

Repotting:
Repot every 3 to 4 years. Keep it potbound to restrict growth.

Pests and Problems:
Leaf drop and loss of lower branches is caused by hot, dry air or insufficient moisture in soil. Waterlogging may also be the culprit.

Dropping of older leaves and lower branches is natural.

Asparagus species
Asparagus fern

The two most popular asparagus plants, *A. plumosa* and *A. sprengeri*, feature delicate, feathery foliage. Although these plants may look like ferns, the tiny leaves are actually flattened stems. *A. sprengeri* has arching 18 to 24 inch stems that are covered with thousands of tiny, inch–long flat needles. *A. plumosa* is a trailing vine with 12 to 18 inch stems, covered with dark green ⅛-inch needles. Both look best displayed in hanging baskets.

These plants have been favorites for generations because they are so easy to care for. Unlike most other ferns, they will tolerate a wide range of temperatures and light levels. Also, they do not require a humid atmosphere and can be easily propagated. To keep the plants bushy, pinch off the ends of the long stems.

Temperature:
Average 68 to 72° days; 60 to 65° nights.

Water:
Keep soil barely moist.

Light:
Bright indirect or curtain filtered sunlight.

Propagation:
Divide thick fleshy roots of old plants any season. Cut the stems to soil level. Fresh new stems will soon grow.

Soil Mix:
All-purpose potting soil or 1 part loam, 1 part peat moss or leaf mold, and 1 part sharp sand.

Repotting:
Anytime plants become overcrowded.

Aspidistra elatior
Cast-iron plant

This is one of the most famous houseplants of the Victorian era, noted for its ability to survive against considerable odds of extreme heat and low light that would be deadly to most other plants. The leaves are oblong, shiny, dark green, and leathery, growing 15 to 30 inches long and 3 to 4 inches wide. They intermingle above a clump of 6-inch-long stems. In spring, dark purple, bell shaped flowers are borne singly at the soil's surface.

This is a slow-growing, long-lasting plant that will respond well to proper attention but will survive poor treatment for a long time. Place out of direct sun in average warmth and water regularly from spring to fall. Reduce water and keep

Asparagus sprengeri

Begonia × rex-cultorum

Aspidistra elatior

cool during the winter when the plant rests. Although the plant can withstand most abuse, it cannot endure soggy soil or frequent repotting.

Temperature:
65 to 75° days; 60 to 65° nights.

Water:
Keep evenly moist spring and summer. Water sparingly during winter.

Light:
Indirect sun. Place in a north-facing window. Tolerant of shade.

Propagation:
In late winter to early spring root crown can be divided.

Soil Mix:
All-purpose mix.

Repotting:
Only every 4 to 5 years in spring when plant is very crowded.

Grooming:
Wash leaves every 2 weeks.

Begonia × rex-cultorum
Rex begonia

Some begonias are grown especially for their blooms. The ones we feature here are grown primarily for their foliage. Rex begonias are the most common foliage type. Large, hairy leaves come patterned in green, red, purple, silver, and white. The plant sometimes reaches a height of 18 inches. The thousands of rex varieties are treasured for their striking colors and distinctive patterned foliage. *B. masoniana*, the iron cross begonia, is another type of rhizomatous begonia. Its green leaves have a puckered surface and unusual brown markings that form a cross in the center.

B. scharffii sports large brown-green leaves with red veins and red undersides.

All of these begonias make terrific plants for window sills or hanging baskets. If placed in good light, but not hot summer sun, in a moderately warm, moist environment, they will thrive. Keep soil moist in spring and summer and fertilize monthly. Many pests bother this plant so inspect frequently, bathe, and treat with appropriate pesticide when necessary.

Temperature:
70 to 75° days; 60 to 65° nights.

Water:
Water regularly during spring and summer. Keep barely moist in fall and winter.

Light:
Bright indirect light. Place in 4

hours of direct sunlight during fall and winter.

Propagation:
Leaf cuttings can be taken any season. Stem cuttings or root divisions can be made in spring and summer.

Soil Mix:
All-purpose mix.

Repotting:
In spring repot crowded plants.

Pests and Problems:
Treat mildew with fungicide. Remove insects by washing plant or spraying with appropriate pesticide.

Brassaia actinophylla
Schefflera, Umbrella tree

This tree is also known as *Schefflera actinophylla*. It is a fast-growing evergreen that can grow to be 8 feet tall. Its common name, the umbrella tree, derives from the glossy green leaflets that spread out like the sections of an umbrella. The leaves of young plants are 2 to 3 inches wide with 3 to 5 leaflets; eventually the leaves grow to be 18 inches across, composed of 16 leaflets. This elegant tree adds a grand touch to any interior.

This is a hardy, easy-to-care-for plant that can tolerate a certain amount of neglect. Place the plant in a bright spot and the container on top of a saucer of gravel with water to maintain humidity. Fertilize monthly with a mild solution of 5-10-5 fertilizer and water when the soil becomes dry.

Brassaia actinophylla

Temperature:
70 to 80° days; 65 to 70° nights.

Water:
Water thoroughly when soil is moderately dry.

Light:
Bright indirect light, but it will benefit from 4 hours of direct sunlight daily.

Propagation:
By air layering in spring.

Soil Mix:
All-purpose mix.

Repotting:
Repot when plant is crowded, any season.

Grooming:
Give the plant an occasional shower.

Pests and Problems:
Highly susceptible to spider mites.

Caladium species

Chlorophytum comosum

Cissus rhombifolia

Caladium species
Caladium

Dozens of varieties of caladium with different leaf patterns and colorings all can create a splendid display of color, sure to rival any flowering plant. Masses of paper thin, spearhead shaped leaves 12 to 24 inches long are borne on long stalks. The exquisite foliage of this perennial dies back for a 4-month period during dormancy. *C. bicolor* features wide red leaves bordered with green, 14 inches long and 6½ inches wide. *C. humboldii* is a miniature plant with light green leaves splotched with white.

Attention to a few basic needs will reward you with vibrant healthy caladiums. Bright indirect light or curtain filtered sunlight is best. Keep the pot on a humidifying tray and mist daily during the growing periods. Warmth is essential; temperatures should never dip below 70° during the day.

Temperature:
75 to 80° days; 65 to 70° nights.

Water:
Water regularly during growing season. Allow to dry out in late fall.

Light:
Bright indirect light or curtain filtered direct sunlight.

Propagation:
In the fall, after the plant dries out, take tubers from the pot and store in dry peat moss at 50 to 60° for 2 months. In the spring divide the tubers and plant one tuber per 5-inch pot in potting soil. Do this in a moist atmosphere with temperatures in the upper 70s. When shoots appear, gradually adjust to normal environment.

Soil Mix:
All-purpose mix.

Repotting:
Each year in the spring.

Grooming:
Trim faded foliage during the growing period. Cut off dead foliage in fall as the plant dies back.

Chlorophytum comosum
Spider plant

The familiar spider plant has been grown indoors since nearly 200 years ago when Goethe, the German writer, brought the plant inside due to his fascination with its habit of producing miniature plants on shoots. The spider plant can grow to be a rotund 3 feet tall. Wiry stems up to 5 feet long, bearing plantlets, spring forth among grassy green, arching leaves striped with yellow or white. This plant is perfect for a hanging basket.

The spider plant will grow in almost any location—sun, shade, dry, or moist. Water freely from spring to autumn and keep in a moderate to cool location. Feed every other week. The plantlets can be left on the stems of the mother plant for a full look or they can be removed for propagation. The plant will produce the most plantlets when slightly potbound.

Temperature:
Moderate 65 to 75° days; 55 to 65° nights.

Water:
Water liberally during growing season, sparingly in winter.

Light:
Bright indirect light but will grow in partial shade.

Propagation:
Divide fleshy roots in spring; pot plantlets any time.

Soil Mix:
All-purpose potting soil.

Repotting:
Whenever plant is overcrowded. Best done in spring.

Pests and Problems:
Pale, limp, and yellowing leaves result from too much heat and too little light. Brown tips come from salts accumulating in the soil. Be sure to leach the soil occasionally to remove this salt buildup. See page 36. Stems will produce *no* plantlets if the plant is too young.

Cissus species

These vigorous, trailing evergreen vines with grapelike tendrils can grow to be 20 feet long. A better hanging plant is hard to find. *C. antarctica*, known as kangaroo vine because it grows by leaps and bounds, has elongated, shiny green leaves. *C. capensis*, oak leaf ivy, has leaves shaped similarly to the oak. *C. discolor*, trailing begonia, the group's showy member, has rosy stems and green leaves flushed silver-rose. *C. rhombifolia* is the popular grape ivy, with dark green leaves formed of 3 leaflets.

Cissus can withstand neglect and poor conditions, making them good office or city inhabitants. Either grow in a hanging container or provide support for climbing and framing. The plant will grow in partial shade but prefers bright indirect light. Feed 2 or 3 times a year. Increase bushiness and control shape by pinching back stems.

Codiaeum variegatum pictum

Coffea arabica

Temperature:
65 to 75° days; 60 to 65° nights.

Water:
Water thoroughly when soil is dry an inch below the surface.

Light:
Bright indirect light or curtain filtered direct light.

Propagation:
Easy, from stem cuttings any time.

Soil Mix:
All-purpose mix.

Repotting:
Repot overcrowded plants any time.

Grooming:
Pinch back stems to control shape.

Pests and Problems:
Provide adequate drainage as this plant is prone to root rot. Whiteflies can be a problem on *C. discolor*.

Codiaeum variegatum
Croton

The varied shapes and exotic colors of the croton's leaves make it an especially attractive plant to feature in a home. Growing to 3 feet high, lance shaped, leathery leaves up to 18 inches long grow from a single stem or trunk. Foliage colors of the many different varieties include red, pink, orange, brown, and white; color markings vary considerably among individual leaves on the same plant. In addition, the plant will sometimes change colors as it matures.

C. variegatum pictum, Joseph's coat, is a popular croton featuring oval, lobed, oaklike leaves in a narrow shrub that usually attains a height of 2 to 4 feet.

Crotons are not easy to grow unless you can satisfy all their environmental needs. Lots of sunshine and a warm location free of drafts are the essentials. The key to success is keeping the plant humid enough to cope with the sun and warm temperatures. Place it on a humidifying tray. Dry air or dry soil will cause the leaves to wither and die rapidly.

Temperature:
75 to 80° days; 65 to 70° nights. Protect from temperatures below 60°.

Water:
Keep soil evenly moist. Water less in the winter.

Light:
Four hours of direct sunlight daily. A southern or western exposure is best. Sunshine enhances the foliage coloring.

Propagation:
In summer root stem cuttings of softwood in moist soil. Air layer any time.

Soil Mix:
All-purpose mix.

Repotting:
In early spring, only if plant is crowded.

Grooming:
Clean leaves and inspect for pests regularly.

Pests and Problems:
Brown tips on leaves are caused by dry air or dry soil. Brown-edged leaves result from low temperatures.

Coffea arabica
Coffee plant

The plant that produces the coffee bean is an evergreen native to Asia and tropical Africa. Extremely popular and adaptable as a container plant, it has a thin main trunk with willowy branches of dense green, oval leaves. Fragrant white flowers and bright red berries appear on the tree during the fall when it is 3 to 4 years old, making it a unique and attractive addition to any room.

The coffee plant makes only a few demands. The soil must always be moist: Dryness will cause severe wilting and possibly permanent damage. Keep it in a warm spot, protected from drafts.

Temperature:
70 to 75° days; 60 to 65° nights; 50° minimum in winter.

Water:
Water soil frequently. Keep soil moist but not soggy.

Light:
Bright indirect light. Southern or western exposures in spring and fall are recommended.

Propagation:
Stem cuttings in summer. Apply bottom heat. Plants can be raised from unroasted coffee beans.

Soil Mix:
All-purpose mix.

Repotting:
Every 2 to 3 years in spring.

Grooming:
Prune the top to increase bushiness.

Coleus hybrida

Dieffenbachia maculata 'Tropic Snow'

Coleus hybrida

Coleus hybrida
Coleus

So richly colored are the leaves of this member of the mint family that many people believe coleus is the most colorful, inexpensive substitute for the croton; as a result it's been tagged the "poor man's croton." Coleus is a fast-growing tropical shrub composed of oval scalloped leaves tapering to a point. The velvety leaves come in a multitude of colors with toothed and fringed margins, depending on the variety. Dark blue or white flowers form in the fall.

These are easy to care for provided you adhere to a few basics. Place coleus in a brightly lit, warm spot. Water the soil regularly and fertilize monthly. Nip flowers when they appear to encourage compact growth and branching; otherwise the plant will become leggy.

Temperature:
75 to 80° days; 65 to 70° nights.

Water:
Keep soil evenly moist. Reduce in winter. Do not use hard water.

Light:
Place in bright indirect light. Protect from high noon sun.

Propagation:
Take stem cuttings in spring or summer. Very easy.

Soil Mix:
All-purpose mix.

Repotting:
Repot when plant becomes potbound.

Grooming:
Pinch tips of shrub to encourage bushy growth. Nip buds of flowers to retard reproductive cycle.

Pests and Problems:
Leaf drop in winter is normal. Leggy stems result from too little light or lack of pinching.

Dieffenbachia
Dieffenbachia; Dumb cane

Touched to the tongue, the sap from the canelike stems of dieffenbachia can cause temporary speechlessness and much pain; thence the name, "dumb cane." This handsome evergreen features a single thick trunk when young, which unwinds into multiple trunks to create a palmlike appearance as the plant matures. Arching, oblong, pointed leaves 10 to 12 inches long spiral around the trunk. *D. picta* 'Rudolph Roehrs' has chartreuse leaves marbled with ivory, divided by a dark green central rib. Mature plants reach ceiling height. For planter and large container decorations, dieffenbachias have few equals indoors all year, or outdoors in warm shade.

With the proper care these plants will thrive indoors. Place in a moderately bright spot; a northern or eastern exposure is fine. Allow soil to dry between thorough waterings; keep air moist always and feed monthly during the growing season. Remove yellowed foliage promptly and wash leaves occasionally.

Temperature:
75 to 80° days; 65 to 70° nights.

Water:
When soil is dry to the touch, water thoroughly. Do not overwater.

Light:
Bright indirect light.

Propagation:
In spring or summer air layer. Protect yourself from burning, poisonous sap.

Soil Mix:
All-purpose mix.

Repotting:
When crowded, repot.

Grooming:
Bathe leaves occasionally and remove withered foliage promptly.

Dizygothica elegantissima
False aralia

This is one of the most graceful plants you can bring indoors. Thin, dark green leaves with lighter veins spread fingerlike into 9 segments with sawtooth edges. You can buy thumb pot seedlings for terrariums, or a mature plant large enough to sit under.

With the right care, this slow grower should cause few problems. It's extremely sensitive to the level of moisture in the soil: Soggy soil is unacceptable, yet a dry rootball will cause the leaves to yellow. Also, this

zygothica elegantissima

Dracaena fragrans 'Massangeana'

Epipremnum aureum

plant does not like being moved around. The key is to provide moist air at all times.

Temperature:
68 to 75° days; 65 to 70° nights.

Water:
Water moderately from April to October. Reduce in winter.

Light:
Bright indirect light. Older plants can endure less light.

Propagation:
Difficult; not recommended.

Soil Mix:
All-purpose mix.

Repotting:
In spring every 2 years. Prefers to be potbound.

Pests and Problems:
Lower leaf drop results from exposure to drafts. The plant is also susceptible to mites.

Dracaena species

These palmlike members of the Lily family feature a single stem with a tuft of swordlike leaves on top. When mature, the tree can reach a height of 10 feet.

Many different varieties are available. Plain green *D. fra-*

grans occasionally yields sprays of fragrant white flowers among its large leaves. *D. god-seffiana* has broad leaves marbled with white and gold and is miniature in comparison to the others. *D. marginata* has red edged thin leaves atop trunks that naturally zigzag and curve. All of these make truly dramatic houseplants whether placed indoors in the living room or outdoors on the porch.

The ease with which dracaenas grow depends on the variety you select to grow. *D. marginata* is the easiest to grow: It can endure shade and low winter temperatures. In general, warmth and abundant light are the keys to strong growth. Keep the soil moist, not soggy, and feed only every 6 months. In spring or summer, stimulate new growth and rejuvenate old plants by cutting back 6 to 8 inches.

Temperature:
75 to 80° days; 65 to 70° nights.

Water:
Keep soil barely moist at all times, but not soggy.

Light:
Bright indirect light or curtain filtered direct sunlight.

Propagation:
Take suckers from plant base, 3-inch stem cuttings, or cut the top off of an old plant in spring or summer. Plant them in regular potting soil. Keep moist.

Soil Mix:
All purpose mix.

Pests and Problems:
Brown tips and yellow edges on leaves are caused by dry air. Surround pot with moist peat. Underwatering or cold drafts may also be the cause.

Brown spots on leaves result from dryness at the roots.

Pale leaves that curve downward with brown edges result from low temperatures.

Yellowing lower leaves is natural in older leaves.

Epipremnum aureum
Pothos; Devil's ivy

Pothos is also known as *Scindapsis aureus*. Sometimes mistaken for a philodendron, this versatile climbing plant will grow in water for months, keep in a planter for years, or, given good moist, rich soil, will frame a window in record time. Pothos, as florists refer to them, feature apple-green heart shaped leaves boldly splashed with creamy white. Silver pothos 'Marble Queen' is creamier than it is white. Both these types require greenhouse-type environments.

Although reputed to be difficult, *E. aureum* actually will do well as long as its needs are met. Keep the plant out of drafts in a warm, well lit, humid location. Let soil dry to the touch between waterings. Pinch out tips to encourage bushiness.

Temperature:
65 to 70° days; 60 to 70° nights. Cooler in winter.

Water:
Water frequently during spring and summer; less in winter.

Light:
Bright indirect light.

Propagation:
Take stem cuttings in spring. Keep soil barely moist and place in dark until rooted.

Soil Mix:
All-purpose mix.

Repotting:
In spring when necessary.

Grooming:
Pinch out growth tips to induce bushiness.

Pests and Problems:
Lack of variegation results from poor light.

Fatsia japonica

Ficus benjamina

Fatshedera

Ficus diversifolia

Fatsia japonica
Japanese aralia

This handsome evergreen foliage plant has bold, lobed leaves of shiny green, occasionally variegated with white. In frost-free climates it can be grown outdoors, but it also makes an excellent contribution to indoor gardens, especially in the North. The smaller plant, *Fatshedera* (aralia ivy or tree ivy), is a hybrid of *Fatsia* and English ivy; it has *Fatsia's* leaves and the growth habit of ivy.

Being both durable and tolerant of many different environments, Japanese aralia is a fast and easy grower. Place it in a cool, well ventilated location with bright light. Wash and mist the leaves regularly and feed every 2 weeks during the growing season or the leaves may yellow due to nitrogen deficiency. The plant rests during winter, so move it to a cool, dry spot. Remove any flower buds that may emerge in the mature plant to prevent it from going into the reproductive cycle. If it begins to look gangly or has misshapen leaves, trim it back to its stalk. New shoots will appear soon.

Temperature:
65 to 70° days; 60 to 65° nights; no warmer than 70° in winter.

Water:
Keep soil evenly moist during growing season. Water sparingly in winter.

Light:
Bright indirect light.

Propagation:
In summer take stem cuttings.

Soil Mix:
All-purpose potting soil.

Repotting:
Prefers to be potbound. Repot in spring every year when roots fill pot.

Grooming:
Clean foliage regularly. Be careful not to bruise tender leaves.

Ficus species
Ficus; Ornamental fig tree

This large, diverse family of over 800 tropical trees and shrubs includes not only the edible fig, *Ficus carica*, but a number of ornamentals perfect for container gardening. Here we discuss some of the favorites for indoors.

Provided with good light, rich, evenly moist soil, and frequent light feeding, ficus will grow well. Guard against overwatering, and protect from cold drafts, dry heat, and sudden changes in environment. If moved to a new location, often the tree will lose most of its leaves and will need a period of adjustment. With care it will flourish again. (See Acclimating New Plants, page 17.)

F. benjamina, the weeping fig, holds a prominent position in the container plant world because it is favored by so many designers. The bark is birchlike with graceful, arching branches loaded with glossy, pointed leaves. It grows from 2 to 18 feet tall.

F. diversifolia, the mistletoe fig, is an interesting miniature upright tree. It grows to a height of 36 inches, bearing many perfect Lilliputian (but inedible) figs. Its small, rounded leaves are flecked with translucent silver. In bright sun the fruits turn red.

F. elastica and the larger leafed *F. e.* 'Decora' are old favorites commonly referred to as rubber plants. They have bold, deep green leaves on stems from 2 to 10 feet tall. *F. e.* 'Variegata' has long, narrow leaves that make a rippling pattern of grass green, metallic gray, and creamy yellow. When

Ficus elastica

Ficus lyrata

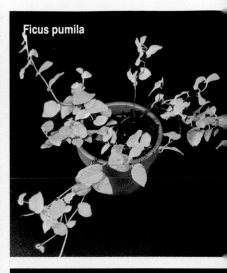

Ficus pumila

Fittonia verschaffeltii var. argyroneura

a rubber plant becomes too lanky, cut off the top and select a side branch to form a new main shoot, or air layer.

F. lyrata (also known as *F. pandurata*) is the fiddleleaf fig, a striking container plant. It has durable papery leaves of deep green in a fiddle shape. The plant can grow from 5 to 10 feet tall.

F. nitida is a similar fig with smaller leaves growing in an upright, compact shape.

F. pumila, the creeping fig, has tiny, heart shaped leaves. This fast-growing trailer is a good plant for hanging baskets or a cascading shelf plant.

Care of Ficus

Temperature:
75 to 85° days; 60 to 65° nights.

Water:
Water thoroughly when soil is dry 2 inches below the soil surface. Use tepid water. Reduce amount in winter.

Light:
Bright light. An eastern or western exposure is best.

Propagation:
By air layering.

Soil Mix:
All-purpose potting soil. *F. pumila* and *F. radicans* like a richer soil and more moisture and shade than the other ficus. Add peat to the soil mix.

Repotting:
Prefers to be potbound. Repot every 3 to 4 years in spring until plant is preferred size or too large to handle.

Grooming:
Clean leaves occasionally.

Pests and Problems:
Check regularly for pests or fungus disease. Yellowing leaf edges and some loss of lower foliage result from underfeeding or is a sign of an insect or fungus problem.

Dry shrivelled leaves in trailing types is caused by too much direct sun.

Fittonia species
Nerve plant; Mosaic plant

The intricately veined, oval leaves of the nerve plant grow semiupright and trail over the sides of their container.

F. verschaffeltii var. *argyroneura* displays a mosaic pattern of white veins, while another variety, *F. v.* var. *pearcei*, has intense red veins against olive-green papery thin backgrounds. These make striking hanging plants and small types are good for terrariums.

Fittonia will thrive in most households. Place in a warm spot that receives some light. A northern or eastern exposure is fine. Let soil dry out between waterings and place on a humidifying tray to provide the key ingredient—ample moisture in the air. Feed monthly during the growing season. During the winter move to a cool spot and water lightly.

Temperature:
70 to 80° days; 60 to 70° nights.

Water:
When soil is dry, water moderately.

Light:
Dim light. A northern or eastern-facing window is best.

Propagation:
In spring take stem cuttings.

Soil Mix:
African violet mix.

Repotting:
Every 2 to 3 years in spring.

Grooming:
Pinch and prune regularly to encourage bushiness.

Hedera helix

Iresine herbstii

Maranta leuconeura

Hedera helix
English ivy

Many plants are called ivy, but the most famous is *Hedera helix*. Countless varieties of this perfect trailing and climbing plant are available: 'Merlon Beauty' has typical English ivy leaves, but smaller. 'Itsy Bitsy' is a tiny variety. Others have the same leaves, but curled, waved, and crinkled. 'Curli-locks' is an example. And some others have color variegation; for example, the yellow-gold and green 'California Gold'. Many will send out aerial roots and climb rough surfaces, such as a brick fireplace wall, or you can use them in large planters as a ground cover. Ivies make excellent hanging baskets and can be trained on espaliers also.

Protected from hot, dry air, English ivy will flourish as long as a few basics are followed. Place it in a cool, bright spot and keep the soil and air moist. During the growing season feed every 2 weeks. Bathe the foliage occasionally. Plants rest in both fall and winter.

Temperature:
60 to 70° days; 50 to 60° nights.

Water:
Keep soil evenly moist, but not soggy.

Light:
Three hours of direct sunlight daily. Southern, eastern, or western exposures are fine.

Propagation:
By division, layering, or stem cuttings.

Soil Mix:
All-purpose potting soil.

Repotting:
Every 2 to 3 years when roots become potbound.

Grooming:
In spring, prune back to encourage bushy growth.

Pests and Problems:
Sparse, spindly growth and dry brittle leaves come from hot temperatures and dry air. Spider mites may also be the problem. Small leaves and too much stem indicate lack of light. Brown leaf tips result from dry air. Green leaves on variegated types result from too little light.

Iresine herbstii
Beefsteak plant; Bloodleaf

The ornamental foliage of this plant is colored an intense, full bodied red, as its common name, bloodleaf, suggests. *I. herbstii* features heart shaped leaves with light red veins. *I. herbstii* 'Aureo-reticulata' produces green leaves tinted with red and lined with yellow veins. The small plants add brilliant accents to groupings of larger plants.

These plants are easy to care for; however, without a good deal of light the leaves pale and the plant becomes leggy, rather than bushy and compact. Water regularly and keep air humid. In the summer, revive your plants with a vacation outdoors.

Temperature:
65 to 70° days; 60 to 65° nights.

Water:
Keep soil evenly moist. Water sparingly in winter.

Light:
Bright light, as much as possible. South-facing window is best.

Propagation:
In spring or summer take stem cuttings.

Soil Mix:
All-purpose potting soil.

Repotting:
In spring if necessary.

Grooming:
Pinch back growing tips to encourage bushier growth.

Maranta leuconeura
Prayer plant

The name "prayer plant" refers to the growth habit of *M. leuconeura kerchoveana*. In the daytime its bronzy marked, satiny foliage lays flat; at night these leaves turn upward, giving the appearance of praying hands. The plant reaches a height of about 8 inches. There are many other varieties as well; all bear spectacular foliage with colored veins and brush strokes of color on backgrounds of white to black.

M. leuconeura massangeana is a showy variety, sometimes called cathedral windows because the foliage is colored similar to stained glass.

Although the prayer plant is fairly easy to grow, some of the less common types are better left for the experienced gardener.

These plants like a warm, humid environment in partial shade. Direct sunlight will cause the leaves to fade. Surround pots with peat moss

Mimosa pudica

Monstera deliciosa

or plant in a grouping to provide the needed humidity. The soil should be moist at all times.

Temperature:
70 to 80° days; 60 to 70° nights; minimum temperature of 55° in winter, through March. Guard against sudden fluctuations in temperature.

Water:
Soil should be kept moist but not soggy. Barely water in winter.

Light:
Moderate light; partial shade is best.

Propagation:
By layering, division, or stem cuttings.

Soil Mix:
African violet mix.

Repotting:
Grows best when potbound. Repot every 2 to 3 years in spring.

Grooming:
Wash leaves and remove withered foliage promptly.

Pests and Problems:
Brown tipped, dry leaves result from dry air. Also check for red spider mite. Yellow lower leaves and curled and spotted upper leaves are caused by underwatering. Limp rotting leaves in winter come from cold, wet environment.

Mimosa pudica
Sensitive plant

Children find the delicate leaves of the sensitive plant fascinating because of their curious habit of folding tightly together when touched, and then slowly unfolding again. The thin branches of leaves, composed of many tiny fernlike leaflets, reach a height of 18 inches. Mature plants will produce tiny pink, puff shaped blossoms but the foliage is not as sensitive as foliage on the younger plants.

These are not difficult to grow in a brightly lit, warm location. Take care not to overwater and feed monthly with a diluted fertilizer. Grow them in 4-inch pots.

Temperature:
75 to 85° days; 65 to 75° nights.

Water:
Water regularly to keep soil moist.

Light:
Bright indirect light.

Propagation:
Sow seeds in spring.

Soil Mix:
All-purpose potting soil.

Repotting:
In spring. Rarely necessary.

Grooming:
Try not to injure the leaves by touching them too often.

Monstera deliciosa
Monstera; Split-leaf philodendron

Found in many homes, *M. deliciosa* climbs and sends out aerial roots that attach to supports or grow to the ground. Stems can reach a length of 6 feet or more and sport large perforated and deeply cut leaves.

These plants are easy to grow as long as you provide a few essentials. Direct the aerial roots into the soil to give support to the weak stem and grow under average room conditions. Keep soil barely moist in winter. Feed every 2 weeks during the growing season.

Temperature:
65 to 75° days; 65 to 70° nights. Not less than 50° in winter.

Water:
Water when soil is dry to the touch. Do not waterlog. Reduce amount in winter.

Light:
Bright indirect light; will tolerate shade.

Propagation:
When plant grows too tall, take stem cuttings from the top. The parent will continue to grow. Another possibility—air-layering. (See page 49.)

Soil Mix:
All-purpose mix.

Repotting:
Prefers to be potbound. Repot every 2 to 3 years in spring.

Grooming:
Wash and polish mature leaves. Guide aerial roots into soil or support. Cut tops of tall plants to limit growth.

Pests and Problems:
Waterlogged soil will cause leaves to weep around edges. Leaves with brown, brittle edges result from dry air. Brown edges and yellowed leaves are a symptom of overwatering or, less frequently, underfeeding. Dropping of lower leaves is normal.

Serious leaf drop results from moving the plant or an abrupt change in environment. Young leaves often have no perforations. Low light also will cause small, unperforated leaves.

Pandanus species

Peperomia species

Pilea species

The profuse number of *Pilea* species available and the ease with which they grow make them popular additions to many homes. Best known is the aluminum plant, *P. cadieri*, which features fleshy stems and silver splashed leaves. *P. microphylla*, the artillery plant, sports tiny fernlike leaves and ejects puffs of pollen when disturbed. Both of these varieties are bushy and reach a height of about 12 inches. Two trailing types are *P. depressa*, creeping Jenny; and *P. nummulariifolia*, creeping Charlie.

These rapid-growing plants are well known for their ability to withstand neglect, although with age they tend to become unattractive. To control the spindly growth of older plants, pinch back stems and repot frequently. Or better yet, each spring grow new plants from the easily rooted cuttings. For the fullest look, put several cuttings in one pot.

Temperature:
68 to 75° days, 65 to 68° nights; not less than 50° in the winter.

Water:
Water thoroughly when soil becomes dry to the touch. Reduce the amount in winter.

Light:
Bright indirect light or slight shade.

Propagation:
Stem cuttings root easily in spring or summer.

Soil Mix:
All-purpose mix.

Pandanus species
Screw pine

Commonly referred to as screw pine because the cornlike, prickly edged leaves spiral upward corkscrew fashion in a compact rosette, *Pandanus* is a tough but graceful plant. Some varieties have white vertical stripes; others have burgundy edges. Aerial roots grow downward, searching for moist soil.

This is an almost foolproof, pest-free specimen to add to your indoor collection. Locate it in a warm spot with moist air. Water frequently from spring to fall, then reduce in winter, leaving the plant mostly dry. Place plant on a humidifying tray. The prickly leaves can injure your hands as well as other plants.

Temperature:
65 to 75° days; 60 to 65° nights.

Water:
Water frequently during growing season.

Light:
Bright light. Protect from direct sun in summer.

Propagation:
Small suckers will appear at base of plant. Remove when they are about 6 inches high. Plant and apply bottom heat.

Soil Mix:
All-purpose potting soil.

Repotting:
Repot overcrowded plants in spring.

Grooming:
Wash foliage occasionally. Train aerial roots into soil.

Peperomia species

The crinkled, heart shaped leaves of peperomia take on a quilted appearance when clumped together in its compact rosette. Spikes of tiny, rat-tail flower heads add an unusual flair to the composition. Most common is *P. sandersi* (also known as *P. argyreia*), the watermelon peperomia. The velvety dark green leaves have a silver-purple sheen in sunlight. There are dozens of varieties to choose from; many make excellent dish garden and terrarium subjects.

These slow-growing plants are well suited to the environment of the average home. Grow in a bright, semishady spot and when the soil feels dry to the touch, water thoroughly.

Temperature:
65 to 75° days; 60 to 70° nights. Cooler in winter.

Water:
When soil feels dry to the touch water thoroughly. Use tepid water.

Light:
Bright spot with partial shade. Protect from direct sunlight.

Propagation:
In spring and summer take stem cuttings.

Soil Mix:
All-purpose soil; can be supplemented with peat moss.

Repotting:
This plant does not like being repotted.

Pests and Problems:
Leaves wilt and drop off suddenly from underwatering. Soil should be slightly dry but do not allow leaves to wilt before watering.

Leaves become soft, wilt, and lose color from overwatering, especially in winter.

lea microphylla

Repotting:
Every year in spring.

Grooming:
Pinch out growing tips to keep plants bushy.

Pests and Problems:
Wilted, discolored leaves result from overwatering. Brown edged leaves usually develop from too little light, or a sudden drop in temperature. Cold air and wet soil in winter will cause leaf drop. However, some leaf shedding in winter is normal. Bare stems should be cut back in spring.

Plectranthus species
Swedish ivy

The waxy, leathery leafed, bright green trailing member of the Mint family, *P. australis*, is commonly known as Swedish ivy, although it is neither from Sweden, nor an ivy. The name was attached because it is such a popular hanging and trailing plant in Scandinavia, seen in windows throughout the country. Spikes of white flowers appear occasionally to complement the foliage. Variegated varieties such as *P. coleoides*, *P. oertendahlii*, and *P. purpuratus* have shadings of silver, purple, and gray-greens, and bear pink or lavender blossoms.

Plectranthus australis

This beautiful trailing plant is fairly tolerant and requires a minimum of care to grow well. Place it in bright light and water regularly.

Temperature:
65 to 72° days; 60 to 70° nights.

Water:
Water regularly, keeping soil moist but not soggy.

Light:
Bright light. Protect from direct sun.

Propagation:
In spring or summer take stem cuttings or divide plant. Plantlets start easily.

Soil Mix:
All-purpose mix.

Repotting:
Repot every 2 to 3 years.

Grooming:
Plant tends to get leggy and unattractive with age. Pinch growth tips for a bushier plant.

Podocarpus macrophyllus
Podocarpus; Japanese yew

A more pleasing compact shrub than *P. macrophyllus* var. *maki* is hard to find for your indoor garden. A group of branches supports spirals of thin, yellow-green leaves, each 3 inches long. As the branches lengthen, they gradually arch downward, becoming less upright. Some species of podocarpus can grow to be 10 feet high.

In the right environment the slow-growing podocarpus will thrive for many years indoors. It's a tolerant plant that prefers cool temperatures and bright filtered light. During the winter, place this plant in an unheated sunporch or other cool room. Warm heat will harm the plant. Control the size of your plant by pinching off the tips. This will encourage branching and enhance the bush shape.

Podocarpus macrophyllus

Temperature:
60 to 65° days; 50 to 60° nights.

Water:
Allow soil to dry between thorough waterings.

Light:
Bright light. An eastern or western exposure is best.

Propagation:
Take tip cuttings in spring or seed.

Soil Mix:
All-purpose mix or 3 parts garden loam and 1 part sand.

Repotting:
This plant likes being potbound. Repot only every 3 to 4 years. Select a container that is not too large for the plant.

Grooming:
Cut back and shape to desired size in early spring.

Sansevieria trifasciata

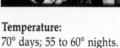

Soleirolia soleirolii

Sansevieria species
*Sansevieria; Snake plant;
Mother-in-law's tongue*

One of the hardiest of all indoor plants is *S. trifasciata*. From a central rosette emerge erect, lance shaped leaves, dark green in color. Golden-yellow striped margins and horizontal bands of gray-green create a striking pattern similar to the coloring of an exotic snake. *S. cylindrica* has round leaves with pointed tips. Mature plants will produce fragrant blooms in pink and white during the spring.

Given proper care, sansevieria will become a showy accent for any indoor decor. Place in a brightly lit, warm spot, and water regularly after soil becomes dry. Overwatering will cause root rot. Fertilize every 2 to 3 months.

Temperature:
75 to 80° days; 65 to 75° nights.

Water:
Water thoroughly when soil feels dry to the touch.

Light:
Bright indirect light. Will tolerate shade.

Propagation:
In spring and summer, divide and pot young offshoots that grow at the plant's base.

Soil Mix:
All-purpose mix or 2 parts loam, 1 part sand, 1 part leaf mold.

Repotting:
Every 3 to 4 years in early spring.

Grooming:
Remove withered foliage and trim off dead flowers.

Soleirolia soleirolii
Baby's tears

Baby's tears, often sold as *Helxine soleirolii*, is a compact creeper composed of tiny, delicate rounded leaves on thin, trailing stems. The plant grows thick and dense and makes a good terrarium ground cover.

This plant loves humidity and grows rapidly in moist, greenhouselike conditions.

Temperature:
70° days; 55 to 60° nights.

Water:
Keep soil moist.

Light:
Bright indirect light. Northern or eastern exposure is best. Will grow in shade.

Propagation:
By division.

Soil Mix:
All-purpose mix.

Syngonium podophyllum
Arrowhead vine

This plant closely resembles its relatives, the climbing philodendrons, both in appearance and care. An unusual feature of Syngonium is the change which occurs in the leaf shape as the plant ages. Young leaves are 3 inches long, arrow shaped, and borne at the end of erect stalks. They are dark green with bold variegation in silvery white. With age the leaves become lobed and the stems acquire a climbing habit. Eventually each leaf fans out into several leaflets; older leaves will sport up to 11 leaflets and turn solid green. All stages of leaf development appear simultaneously on mature plants.

Arrowhead vines do best in a warm, moist environment, protected from direct sunlight. Older climbing stems require support—a moss stick works well. To retain the juvenile leaf form and variegation, prune off the climbing stems and aerial roots as they appear.

Temperature:
Average warmth; at least 60° in winter.

Water:
Keep the soil barely moist at all times. Water less in winter and avoid overwatering.

Light:
Bright indirect light away from direct sun, especially for variegated types.

Propagation:
In spring or summer take stem cuttings.

Soil Mix:
All-purpose potting soil.

Repotting:
Every 2 or 3 years in the spring.

Grooming:
Pinch off long stems at any time to increase branching and encourage more young, variegated leaves.

ngonium podophyllum

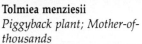

Tolmiea menziesii

Tradescantia albiflora 'Albo vittata'

Tolmiea menziesii
Piggyback plant; Mother-of-thousands

A favorite among children, this popular plant is noted for its unusual leaf growth: The hairy, bright green leaves send out tiny new plantlets at the junction of the leaf and stem. Because so many new plants form, it's sometimes called mother-of-thousands.

These easy-to-grow plants will do fine in a cool, well ventilated spot. Hot, dry air harms the plant. Keep soil moist, feed every two months, and grow in a brightly lit spot. This plant will tolerate the shade. Spider mites thrive on piggyback plants so watch for brown, brittle leaves and treat them immediately.

Temperature:
55 to 70° days; 40 to 55° nights.

Water:
Keep soil evenly moist.

Light:
Bright indirect light.

Propagation:
Leaf cuttings with plantlets root easily anytime.

Soil Mix:
All-purpose potting soil.

Repotting:
Anytime when plant becomes overcrowded.

Grooming:
Pinch off wilted leaves immediately. Prune to shape.

Pests and Problems:
Brown, brittle leaves signal spider mite attack. Treat immediately. Plant was probably too hot and dry.

Tradescantia species
Wandering Jew; Inch plant

This member of the Spiderwort family is grown for its trailing, showy foliage. Leaves alternate along thick, succulent stems. Naturals for hanging baskets or as trailing plants on shelves or window sills, these ornamentals are also welcome additions to groupings of green foliage plants. Sunlight intensifies their colorations.

T. albiflora 'Albo-vittata', *T. albiflora* 'Laekenensis', *T. blossfeldiana*, and *T. navicularis* are small trailers with oval leaves brightly variegated in shades of white, purple, bluegreen, red, bright green, brown, and gold.

These plants are easy to care for and grow rapidly. Place in a bright spot with direct sun; an eastern or western exposure is best. Allow soil to dry between waterings and keep surrounding air moist. Feed every 2 weeks during growing season.

Temperature:
65 to 70° days; 55 to 65° nights.

Water:
Water thoroughly when soil feels dry. Water the plants less often in winter.

Light:
Bright light. Eastern or western exposure is best.

Propagation:
By cuttings or division.

Soil Mix:
All-purpose potting soil.

Repotting:
Each spring when plant is crowded.

Grooming:
Pinch back to encourage bushy growth.

Caryota mitis

Chamaerops humilis

Chamaedorea elegans

Chrysalidocarpus lutescens

Palms

Palms are a consistently popular houseplant. Their graceful fans and rich green color can instill even the coldest northern home with a tropical flair and elegance. This is a large and varied plant family of which only a few are grown indoors. Although they are some of the most expensive plants you can buy, they are well worth the investment. As tolerant plants, they adapt well to the limited light and controlled temperatures of homes. You can save money by purchasing small young plants that will slowly grow to a mature size.

Some types will flourish in the home for decades.

Most members of the Palmae family are easy to care for care for and prefer similar growing conditions. During the spring and summer growing season, water plants heavily and feed them once a month. Reduce water and stop feeding in winter. Protect from dry air and direct sunlight, especially if you move your palm outdoors. Do not prune palm trees unless an old branch dies naturally. Unlike most plants, the life support systems of palms are located directly in the tip of the stalk. Pinching out

this tip or cutting off the newest frond below its point of attachment to the trunk will eliminate all new growth.

Caryota mitis
Fishtail palm

This large palm features a thick trunk and many spreading branches, each laden with fans of dark green leaves. The ribbed texture of the leaves and wedge shape evoke the palm's common name.

Chamaedorea elegans
Parlor palm

This palm, also known as *Neanthe bella*, features handsome light green fronds. Sometimes it bears bunches of small yellow fruit near the base of the trunk. It is a relatively small palm, growing to a height of 6 feet—perfect for entryways, living rooms, or shady decks.

Chamaerops humilis
European fan palm

Stiff, severely cut leaves form fans 1 foot wide atop 4-foot stems when the European fan

Howea forsterana

Phoenix roebelenii

Rhapis excelsa

palm reaches full maturity. The fans grow to varying heights and at different angles, rising from a rough, black trunk. This is a striking plant for any room.

Chrysalidocarpus lutescens
Areca palm; Butterfly palm

This is a medium-size, slow-growing palm. It features a cluster of thin, canelike stems with arching fronds and strap shaped, shiny, green leaflets.

Howea forsterana
Kentia palm

This popular palm grows to be a very large tree outdoors in

nature. Indoors, *Howea* will rarely pass 7 or 8 feet. Feather shaped leaves arch outward from sturdy branches to create a full appearance. Outside in bright light the leaves will scorch easily, so take care to place in the shade.

Phoenix roebelenii
Pygmy date palm

This date palm is a dwarf palm, growing to a height of 4 feet. A more delicate palm, it has a straight, symmetrical shape composed of branching, narrow-leaf fronds with a pendulous habit. Like the others, it requires a minimum of attention.

Rhapis excelsa
Large lady palm

Also called *R. aspera*, this large palm features 6 to 12-inch-wide fans composed of 4 to 10 thick, shiny leaves. The leaves occur at the ends of thin, arching stems along a brown, hairy main trunk.

Care of Palms

Temperature:
60 to 70° days and nights. Cooler in winter, but not less than 50°.

Water:
Water liberally in spring and summer. Good drainage is important.

Light:
Bright light, but they will grow in shade.

Propagation:
From seed, but it's difficult.

Soil Mix:
All-purpose mix or a mixture of 1 part all-purpose mix and 1 part peat moss.

Repotting:
Not necessary very often. Repot in late spring, early summer.

Grooming:
Wash leaves to control spider mites and sucking insects. Slice off old bases of leaves at the very bottom of the trunk, taking care not to cut into the trunk.

Philodendron hastatum

Philodendron oxycardium

Philodendron 'Red Emerald'

Philodendrons

No other group of plants has made itself such a prevalent addition to our homes. The leathery, glossy leaves cut in unique shapes, as well as the range of sizes and types—evergreens, vines, shrubs, and trees—will allow you to select one in tune with the look you want to achieve. And you don't have to worry about providing perfect growing conditions; originally from South American tropical forests, philodendrons are strong, tolerant plants that don't need a lot of sunshine.

The 200 different species break down into 2 types. The "climbers" are most commonly grown in the home. The name is a bit of a misnomer, though: None of them climb very well, so they must be tied to supports. Aerial roots extend from their upper leaves to seek nourishment. These should be tied up or directed to the ground.

The other type, "non-climbers," can become enormous plants 6 to 8 feet high. Their leaves, of varying shapes, extend from self-supporting trunks. These are great for offices or large, high-ceiling rooms.

Practicing a few basic techniques will keep your philodendron healthy and thriving. Place the plant in bright light; it doesn't need direct sunlight to grow well. Water regularly to maintain a moist soil. About once a month the leaves should be washed. An undersized pot, low temperatures, or poor drainage will cause leaves to yellow and drop. If lower leaves yellow and drop on the climbing types don't be overly alarmed; it's usually natural. The following are popular in many homes.

Philodendron bipinnatifidum
Twice-cut philodendron;
Fiddle-leaf philodendron

The deeply cut, star shaped leaves of this plant are very large in size. This is a non-climbing type, so it needs no supports.

Philodendron gloriosum

Velvety leaves are shaped like hearts and dappled with red and cream. This is a very full-looking climber covered with leaves.

Philodendron hastatum
Spade-leaf philodendron

This philodendron is a lush evergreen climbing vine with aerial roots. Deeply veined, bright green leaves take the shape of giant spearheads, 8 to 12 inches long. Older plants will produce perfumed tubular blossoms similar in appearance to calla lilies.

Philodendron oxycardium
Heart-leaf philodendron

This vigorous climber composed of many long, glossy, deep green leaves is the most popular one grown in the United States. It is also known as *Philodendron cordatum.* Train it on a column, frame a window with it, or hang it from a beamed ceiling. This plant does fine in the shade.

Philodendron pertusum
Split-leaf philodendron

See "Foliage Houseplants," *Monstera deliciosa,* page 83.

Philodendron 'Red Emerald'

Red stems are topped with bright green, yellow veined, spear shaped leaves on this 'Red Emerald' philodendron. This is a climber.

ilodendron selloum

Agave species

Aloe variegata

Philodendron selloum
Lacy tree philodendron

This is another non-climbing, cut-leaf philodendron. As the plant ages, the cuts become more severe and cause the leaves to ruffle. This plant is often used to decorate office buildings.

Care of Philodendron

Temperature:
Average warmth, not less than 55° in winter.

Water:
Keep soil evenly moist, not soggy.

Light:
Bright indirect light.

Propagation:
Take stem cuttings in summer or air-layer climbing types. Provide warmth.

Soil Mix:
All-purpose potting mix.

Repot:
About every 2 to 3 years pot up in spring.

Grooming:
Place aerial roots in soil so upper leaves can receive nourishment or tie them to plant supports. Leaves will collect dust, so clean periodically.

Pests and Problems:
It is natural for most philodendrons to drop lower leaves.

Succulents

A succulent is a plant that stores water in its stems or leaves. These plants have mastered the art of water conservation. By reducing their leaf surface in order to cut down on water loss from transpiration, and by storing water in their stems or leaves, succulents can control both the amount of water they need and the amount they use.

Succulents are generally easy to care for and are a good starting point for beginning gardeners. Despite the many different types of succulent plants, they require generally the same care. To grow well they need a porous, well-draining soil, lots of sunshine, good air circulation, and plenty of water. During the winter they must lie dormant in a cool, dry environment. This rest time is essential if you want your plants to

bloom the following season. In summer, revitalize the plants by moving them outdoors.

Here we describe some succulents excellent for indoor culture. For a more complete guide, see Ortho's *The World of Cactus and Succulents*.

Agave species

These succulents feature straplike leaves in rosettes that grow from 3 inches to 8 feet when mature. *A. americana*, the century plant, has large triangular leaves with saw-toothed edges. White to yellow-green flowers are borne on long stalks from the center of the rosette. All agaves flower only once, after which the individual rosette dies. The agave is very easy to grow. It requires a large pot and plenty of water

and fertilizer during its active growing season.

Aloe species

There is a great diversity among the plants in this genus. *A. aristata*, the torch plant or lace aloe, is a dwarf species that features stemless rosettes edged with soft white spines or teeth. In winter, it bears orange-red flowers. *A. barbadensis* (also known as *A. vera*), the medicine plant or burn aloe, is most widely known for the juice of its leaves which people use to treat minor burns. It is a stemless plant with green leaves and yellow flowers. *A. variegata*, the tiger aloe, displays white spotted, boat shaped, green leaves in triangular rosettes. Pink to dull red flower clusters appear intermittently throughout the year.

Beaucarnea recurvata

Crassula ovata

Ceropegia woodii

Echeveria species

Faucaria tigrina

Beaucarnea species
Bottle palm

Outdoors the bottle palm eventually grows into a tree 20 feet tall, but as a houseplant it will stay a manageable size. *B. recurvata*, the elephant-foot tree or ponytail palm, is most often distinguished by the base of the gray-brown trunk, which resembles a large onion when the plant is young. Long, thin green leaves arch out all around the apex of the stem, creating a fountainlike effect. Insignificant flowers are beige and borne in summer.

Ceropegia woodii
Rosary vine

The rosary vine sports trailing stems of small, heart shaped, dark green leaves marbled with white. Tiny flowers with bulbous bases and black petals joined at the tips appear all along the vines. Most bloom in the summer, but a few appear in the spring and fall.

Rosary vine makes an attractive, especially interesting hanging plant for interiors. Give it more water than you would other succulents.

Crassula argentea
Jade plant

This compact, treelike succulent has stout, branching limbs with oblong, fleshy leaves, 1 to 2 inches long. In direct sun, the smooth, leathery, dark green leaves become tinged with red. This popular plant ranges in height from 1 to 5 feet.

Echeveria species
Echeveria; Hen and chicks

All echeverias have in common a rosette form. Their greatly varied leaf color ranges from pale green through deep purple. Many are luminous pink. *E. elegans*, the pearl echeveria, forms a tight rosette of small whitish green leaves. Rose colored flowers tipped with yellow are borne on pink stems in spring or summer. These are great for dish gardens. 'Morning Light' is a hybrid which features rosettes of beautiful, luminous pink foliage.

Echeverias generally do well with more water, fertilizer, and a richer soil than most succulents. Exposure to light has a direct effect upon the intensity of foliage color. If stems become leggy, the plant can be cut down and rerooted.

Faucaria species
Tiger's jaws

This popular succulent is very short stemmed and takes its common name from triangular leaves with small teeth along their margins. The leaves grow in small, low clumps, ranging in color from blue green to olive green, often with spotting on the skin. *F. tigrina* has gray-green skin with white dots. *F. tuberculosa* has dark green leaves with small white bumps on the upper side. Both sport yellow to white flowers, similar to dandelions, during the summer. This plant is great for beginners to try.

Kalanchoe blossfeldiana

Lithops species

Sedum morganianum

Senecio rowleyanus

Kalanchoe species

One of the more popular succulents for pot growing, kalanchoes are grown for both their flower and their leaf interest. *K. beharensis*, the felt plant, features large triangular leaves, covered with brown felt, that curve and wave to create a busy look. Pink flowers appear in the spring. *K. blossfeldiana*, flaming katy, produces brilliant heads of scarlet flowers on thin stems 15 inches high. Shiny green oval leaves are tinged with red. *K. tomentosa*, the panda plant, grows to 15 inches. Plump leaves covered with furlike silvery hairs branch from the central stem. The pointed leaves are tipped with rust brown bumps. Indoors this species rarely flowers.

Lithops
Living stones

Often called living stones because of its close resemblance both in shape and coloring to small rocks, *Lithops* grows in stemless clumps of paired leaves approximately 1 to 2 inches in diameter. In November, yellow to white dandelion shaped flowers emerge from between the leaves.

Sedum morganianum
Donkey's tail; Burro's tail

This sedum, commonly called donkey's tail, is a trailing, slow-growing succulent. Light gray to blue-green leaves are ½ to 1 inch long, oval, and plump. The 3 to 4-foot-long trailing stems, covered with clusters of these leaves, create a braided or ropelike effect. This plant is ideal for hanging containers. Locate it where it won't be disturbed, because leaflets break off easily. Also, don't be alarmed by the powdery bluish dust covering the leaves; it's called *bloom* and is also found on plums.

Senecio rowleyanus
String-of-beads

The string-of-beads has hanging stems that bear ½-inch spherical leaves. These unusual leaves look like light green beads with pointed tips and have a single translucent band across them. Small fragrant white flowers appear in winter.

Care of Succulents

Temperature:
70 to 80° days; cool 65° nights.

Water:
Water thoroughly when the soil feels dry a half-inch below the soil surface.

Light:
Bright light. A south-facing exposure on a window sill is fine. Plants moved outside should be placed in shade.

Propagation:
Cuttings and offsets root easily. Dust the exposed cut with fungicide. Dry the offset or cutting for a few days until a callus is formed on the wound, then plant in appropriate soil mix and keep barely moist.

Soil Mix:
Cactus mix or 1 part coarse sand or pumice, 1 part potting soil, and 1 part leaf mold.

Repotting:
Only repot every 3 to 4 years, when essential. Use a shallow pot rather than a deep one.

Pests and Problems:
Root rot results from soggy soil. Stem and leaf rot come from cool, damp air. Leaves wilt and discolor from too much water, especially in winter. Brown dry spots are caused by underwatering. Soft brown spots indicate leaf spot disease.

INDEX

Common names for plants are listed in this index and cross-referenced to the proper botanical name. Common names vary from region to region, and space has limited us to those most widely used. Italic page numbers refer to pages with photographs of the plant.